GOVERNING PUBLIC-PRIVATE PARTNERSHIPS

Governing Public-Private Partnerships

JOSHUA NEWMAN

McGill-Queen's University Press
Montreal & Kingston • London • Chicago

ISBN 978-0-7735-4998-2 (cloth)
ISBN 978-0-7735-4999-9 (paper)
ISBN 978-0-7735-5000-1 (ePDF)
ISBN 978-0-7735-5001-8 (ePUB)

Legal deposit second quarter 2017
Bibliothèque nationale du Québec

Printed in Canada on acid-free paper that is 100% ancient forest free
(100% post-consumer recycled), processed chlorine free.

McGill-Queen's University Press acknowledges the support of the
Canada Council for the Arts for our publishing program. We also
acknowledge the financial support of the Government of Canada
through the Canada Book Fund for our publishing activities.

Library and Archives Canada Cataloguing in Publication

Newman, Joshua, 1978–, author
    Governing public-private partnerships / Joshua Newman.

Includes bibliographical references and index.
Issued in print and electronic formats.
ISBN 978-0-7735-4998-2 (cloth). – ISBN 978-0-7735-4999-9 (paper). –
ISBN 978-0-7735-5000-1 (ePDF). – ISBN 978-0-7735-5001-8 (ePUB)

    1. Public-private sector cooperation – Management. I. Title.

HD3871.N49 2017   336   C2017-901523-0
                                          C2017-901524-9

This book was typeset by True to Type in 10.5/13 Sabon

Contents

Acknowledgments

As much as all the faults in this text are my own responsibility and no one else's, I am indebted to a number of people for any merits that the reader can find. First, I would like to thank Anthony Perl, Michael Howlett, and Brian Head for their invaluable guidance and mentorship over the time that this material made its sojourn from research to book.

Likewise, I am grateful to my academic colleagues and fellow staff members at Simon Fraser University, the University of Queensland, and Flinders University, whose help, encouragement, and friendship made this work much easier and more enjoyable than it would have been otherwise.

I would like to thank my parents for their seemingly unlimited support, which they somehow managed to offer even over great distances.

And of course, my wife, Sothea, without whom none of this could have been possible.

GOVERNING PUBLIC-PRIVATE PARTNERSHIPS

1

Introduction

With the transition away from Keynesian economic management that occurred in the 1980s and 1990s, and with the rapid and easy transnational movement of capital and information often referred to as globalization, the modern democratic state finds itself operating in a world that is converging on a mode of *governance* that differs from the conventional methods of *government* that had been prevalent in Western democracies since the Great Depression. From one point of view, the government's role has changed from one of control to one of "steering" (Mayntz 1993), in that hierarchical government with an independent and process-oriented bureaucracy has been replaced by a system in which the formulation and implementation of public policy is decentralized and is often delegated in part or in whole to non-governmental actors. From this perspective, governance is about how "governments and non-government actors can democratically exert some influence, control and coordination" and effectively steer society (Pierre and Peters 2000, 3). Attitudes about the authority and roles of the state in the international sphere have shifted; the domestic authority of state governments within their own borders has been, in many instances, delegated and decentralized, while remaining powers have been further centralized by state executives; and non-governmental groups and private sector firms are taking a more prominent role in the delivery of formerly public services.[1]

---

1 Following Vining and Weimer (1990, 3), I will take "public services" to include goods as well as services.

In this era of governance, the precise role of the state has become unclear. Marketization, privatization, deregulation, increased competition, outsourcing, contracting out, and mixed models of delivery have resulted in a much greater involvement of the private for-profit sector (and, to a lesser extent, the private non-profit sector) in public service delivery. With this level of delegated authority, and with so many actors involved, little is known about what is required of the state in ensuring successful, sustainable, equitable, and accountable public services for its citizenry. How can the state contribute to sustaining and improving standards of living in the modern era of governance? Should the public sector – a term that will need to be more precisely defined – be more involved, or less? What, ultimately, is the state's responsibility in delivering services to the public?

This book addresses a small but vital component of these questions, by focusing on one increasingly popular instrument of governance: the public-private partnership. Public-private partnerships (also called P3s or PPPs[2]) are a family of alternative service delivery arrangements in which governments and other public sector agencies enter into long-term contractual agreements with private corporations for the delivery of public services. P3s are controversial mechanisms of service delivery: while proponents claim that these partnerships bring an antidote of economic efficiency to the government's tendency toward waste, critics allege that the downsides of P3s – such as contracts that can supersede legislation, profit-driven decision making, and increased user fees – outweigh their purported advantages. However, in the midst of this ongoing debate, governments in the developed and developing worlds are engaging in public-private partnerships at an accelerating pace. And while international best practices in P3 governance continue to evolve, the state's precise role in promoting, supporting, and managing these partnerships is still not completely clear.

In order to address the questions raised above, I will examine two cases of public-private partnership in transportation: the Canada Line in Vancouver, Canada, and the Sydney Airport Rail

2 I prefer to use "P3," as it is the form that is easiest to say out loud. However, many authors continue to use "PPP" as an abbreviation.

Link in Sydney, Australia. While such a small sample cannot allow for statistically significant or universally generalizable conclusions, there is still a tremendous amount that can be learned from these examples because of their capacity for a most-similar-systems case study. The Canada Line and the Sydney Airport Link share a remarkable number of technical, contextual, and organizational similarities, yet the Canada Line has been a resounding success while the Airport Link suffered from governance failure. By comparing these two cases it is possible to tease out some factors that can contribute to failure and others that can support success in public-private partnerships. More to the point, the actions and inactions of the governments and the public sector agencies involved in these two cases provide some intriguing lessons for governments contemplating future P3 projects.

PUBLIC-PRIVATE PARTNERSHIPS AND THE STATE

Public-private partnerships have gained considerable support in recent years. Arguments in favour of P3s often refer to them as the "best of both worlds" (United Nations 2008, iii), a union of private sector efficiency and public sector accountability that is superior to either sector acting alone. P3s have been lauded for their ability to use private finance for public investment, which supporters see as a means of injecting private capital into the public budget, thereby reducing the public's tax burden and freeing up the government's financial resources for other, more pressing demands (Telliford 2009). They are also frequently promoted as being able to add a high degree of efficiency to public service development and delivery, including technical innovation, budget control, and time management, that will result in major cost savings (Poschmann 2003). From the other side of the table, P3s are seen by private corporations as a secure, long-term investment that in many cases is guaranteed (or, at least, protected) by the government (TD Bank Financial Group 2006, 11).

In spite of the enthusiasm with which some governments have embraced public-private partnerships, P3s do not always produce the fantastic outcomes that are attributed to them in theory. Spectacular failures – from both a financial and a social perspective – have been documented in several countries. Advocates of P3s will often point to intrusion from the public sector, such as over-regulation, micromanagement, and political interference, as key factors contributing to failure in P3s (Pongsiri 2002, 490–1; Zhang 2005, 7). Much of the literature that deals with enhancing the use of P3s is predominantly concerned with how governments can improve incentives for the private sector to enter into partnership arrangements (e.g., Abdel Aziz 2007), but not nearly enough attention has been paid to the role that governments can play in participating in, or even managing, the partnerships themselves. While there is a sizeable body of research dealing with the role of the government in collaborative governance arrangements between the public and private sectors (e.g., Bryson et al. 2006), this research has not been specifically extended to public-private partnerships as much and as often as the recent growth in popularity of P3s would warrant (for a discussion on the difference between general collaborative governance and public-private partnership, see Ansell and Gash 2008, 548).

In any case, the lack of discussion of an activist state in P3 governance should not be surprising. The logic of public-private partnerships is based on a presumption that to improve the quality and reduce the cost of public service delivery, some degree of government needs to be removed from the equation. According to one point of view, government-run projects are usually delivered late and over-budget, because governments lack the profit incentives of the market that induce private companies to minimize budgets and schedules (Grimsey and Lewis 2005). P3s – and in a broader sense, all alternative governance arrangements – are seen by many as a way to allow governments to replace their own worst qualities, such as a slow and dense bureaucracy, budget maximization, and political conflict, with the efficiencies and innovative qualities of the profit-driven private sector (Pongsiri 2002; Zhang 2005; TD Bank Financial Group 2006).

Nonetheless, the state has not yet been made obsolete. Governments in developed countries continue to be the primary force in policy formulation and implementation. In fact, even for supporters of alternative service delivery, the necessity of government participation is axiomatic. For example, P3s are seen as being superior to full privatization, because the presence of the public sector adds an increased component of accountability to the public (Pongsiri

2002, 491). This presents an inherent conflict for governance, as governments are perceived simultaneously as the problem and as the solution to improving public service delivery.

There is, therefore, much uncertainty about how the state can best participate in the delivery of goods and services to the public in an era in which multiple public and private sector entities share many responsibilities. If the supposed need for public sector accountability must be reconciled with the perceived need to improve public sector efficiency, is there a level of government participation that will achieve this reconciliation? If that happy medium is not reached, will governance then "fail"? The precise role of the public sector in ensuring successful implementation of policy through the use of P3s and other alternative service delivery instruments is not sufficiently understood, because the research focus to date has been on removing the perceived shortcomings of government from public service delivery, and not on the requisite actions of the state in ensuring success. The state, of course, does have a role to play in formulating and implementing public policy for service delivery; few observers recommend completely eliminating the government in this regard. The challenge is to define that role and its associated level of engagement in governance.

DEFINING SOME IMPORTANT CONCEPTS

The term "private sector" is somewhat intuitive, and in this book I will use it in its traditional sense to refer collectively to private corporations operating in competitive markets or under monopolistic conditions. It should be noted that most not-for-profit organizations also technically belong to the "private" sector, in that these organizations are not owned by the government and are not usually an extension of the state. However, as there is an obvious distinction between these two types of private organizations – namely, the presence or absence of the pursuit of profit – many authors tend to separate them by referring to not-for-profit organizations collectively as the nonprofit sector or the "third" sector (Brock 2005; Webb 2005). I will also employ this convention, and so "private sector" as it is used in this book will refer exclusively to for-profit private corporations.

"Public sector" is a much more ambiguous term, mainly because it comprises so many disparate entities, from elected bodies to corporations. For example, in casual conversation (and frequently in academic writing, as well), the word "government" is often used to refer jointly to the political executive and the bureaucracy, when there is clearly an important distinction to be made between elected decision makers and appointed administrators. Moreover, in modern democracies there are numerous other organizations that belong to the state, such as state-owned corporations, regulatory bodies, autonomous public agencies, independent commissions, the judiciary, and so on.

In general, it is extremely difficult to be precise when discussing the public sector, because responsibilities overlap, powers are concurrent, and stakeholders can hold multiple identities. For instance, in the Vancouver case to be examined in this book, the Canada Line P3 project was managed by a state-owned corporation, which was wholly owned by a statutory agency responsible to a provincial government. Furthermore, the City of Vancouver was a major collaborator in the execution of the project, but its municipal government, while mainly autonomous in its day-to-day operations, is entirely under the legislative jurisdiction of the province (organizational relationships for the Canada Line and the Airport Link will be discussed in more depth in chapter 4). It is therefore difficult to discuss the "government" that was responsible for the Canada Line with any meaningful distinction between the various agencies that were involved, including the provincial executive, the provincial legislature, the Ministry of Transportation, the regional transportation authority, and several other organizations with delegated responsibilities. In this book, I will attempt as much as possible to be precise when referring to agencies that are under the purview of the state, but ambiguities will necessarily arise due to the complicated nature of the relationships between these organizations. For the sake of simplicity, I will sometimes use "public sector" as an umbrella term that comprises all entities for which the state is directly or indirectly responsible.

There are nearly infinite ways for the public and private sectors to collaborate, which makes obtaining a specific and universal definition of public-private partnerships somewhat elusive. Partnership formats and acronyms abound, such as BOOT ("build-own-operate-transfer") and DBFO ("design-build-finance-operate"). Although these names are intended to signify particular financial and legal arrangements between public and private sector entities, the concepts they are meant to convey are overlapping and definitions are often inconsistent in both industry and in academia. What is clear – especially from attempts to catalogue the various names used to refer to formats of P3 arrangements (e.g., Siemiatycki 2006, 138; United Nations 2008, 2–4; Koppenjan and Enserink 2009, 285–6) – is that the degree of public ownership of assets, the percentage of private capital investment, and the nature of the risks assigned to the various entities involved in a P3 project can all vary from project to project. The quantity and arrangement of these ingredients determine the format for a particular project, and they are employed according to the idiosyncratic requirements of the public sector and private sector proponents involved in that project.

Therefore, while a precise definition of public-private partnership may seem desirable, assembling a list of all the possible P3 arrangements would be a difficult and tedious task. There is a continuous spectrum of public ownership, capital investment, and risk allocation that could be supplied for any individual public service project, so these are not activities that can be easily compartmentalized into categories with clearly defined boundaries. A more constructive way to view P3s is as a family of partnership modes, all designed to allow the private sector to deliver goods and services to the public on behalf of the state (Hodge and Bowman 2004, 203). Public-private collaboration is therefore best seen as a spectrum of integration, from purely state-controlled supply on the one hand to complete divestiture to the private sector on the other.

Nonetheless, there are some features that are common to different P3s. All P3s involve some sharing of responsibility between the public and private sectors, as well as some sharing of the risks and rewards of the project in question. While different P3 projects will apportion responsibility, risk, and reward differently, in all cases these three elements will fall in some arrangement to both the public and private sector partners. It is this sharing of responsibility, risk, and reward that creates challenges for P3 governance, mainly because the goals of the government and the goals of a private corporation are not often aligned. Most often, the objective of government will be to solve some political or social problem, perceived or real. For the private sector, the main objective is profit. In many cases – such as supplying public transit to low density neighbourhoods, providing affordable housing for low income families, or dealing with drug dependence – social objectives may not be profitable. In other examples, private corporations involved in service delivery may oppose expanding a program if the expansion will be costly or if it will provide subsidized services that compete with similar services offered at a higher standard rate. In all cases, the private sector partner in a P3 arrangement will object to altering a profitable course of action, even if it means achieving a desirable political or social goal.

Given the private sector's attention to profit, it is no surprise that the vast majority of research on public-private partnerships – academic or otherwise – is concerned with economic aspects and outcomes of the P3 arrangement. However, economic considerations are only one part of the story. The other, untold, story of P3s involves the effectiveness of partnerships as an instrument for achieving policy goals and for attaining specific social outcomes; there is a world of activity that is of great relevance to public policy and to which economic concerns are secondary.

In current Western political culture, in news reports, and in public debate it has become common to conflate economic and social matters. Public projects are spoken of in terms of cost savings, "value for money," and contributions to economic growth, while inequality, standards of living, and other social issues are less prominent themes. More often than not, good policy is seen by the public and by the political elite as necessarily being low-cost or revenue-generating. Modern debates on immigration (Burns and Gimpel 2000; Corden 2003, 9), health care reform (Bauch 2010; Brody 2010; Gregg 2015), and child care (Thériault 2006), among others, often center around economic factors even when the greater issues carry important implications for social well-being that go beyond simple matters of cost, finance, and economic growth. Of course, the financing of public services and their contributions to economic output are matters of critical importance;

nevertheless, the financial goals of a service and its social objectives are frequently two very different things.

As Drucker (1974, 45) observes, there is a difference between effectiveness, which can be a non-economic descriptor, and efficiency, which is necessarily economic: effectiveness describes the achievement of a specific goal, and efficiency is achieving that goal at the lowest possible cost. In the business world, although these two things may be separate (effectiveness, for instance, might require finding the right market for a new product while efficiency might require a factory to assemble the product cheaply), they can both be measured by the same outcome: profit.

In the public sector, however, this is not the case. Social outcomes rarely have an empirical monetary value. Efficiency, in theory, ought to be measured by the difference between the benefits of output and the costs of input (Self 1977, 264), but while the input costs of public programming may be quantified, benefits to society are difficult to measure in financial terms. In other words, social "profit" has no economic meaning, so public sector effectiveness and efficiency must be measured in separate ways (and by different people as well, since social outcomes are gauged by policy analysts and program costs are measured by accounting departments). However, the demands, strategies, and goals of public policy effectiveness – as well as the consequences of ineffective policies – are relevant to politics and to society, and require a separate treatment from economic analysis. Many public policies, such as providing cancer treatment, addressing homelessness, reducing smoking rates, limiting exposure to toxic substances like bisphenol A, and responding to natural disasters, will require social and political decisions that are quite separate from questions of economic efficiency. On the other side of the coin, some projects, like Russia's annexation of Crimea, can be economically efficient but do not necessarily produce quality social outcomes (Barry 2014; Kazatchkine 2014).

Accordingly, while economic analyses of public-private partnerships are plentiful, with both theoretical treatments and empirical studies well represented in the academic literature (e.g., Poschmann 2003; Ohemeng and Grant 2008; Shaoul 2009), alone they are insufficient for a complete understanding of the dynamics of governance of P3s. Yet there are very few studies of P3 governance that are primarily non-economic, and the majority of these studies are highly theoretical (see Hodge and Bowman 2004 for example). There exists only a sparse population of scholarly works examining non-economic aspects of public-private partnerships from an empirical perspective (see Klijn and Teisman 2004 for example).

This gap in the literature may be due to the challenging nature of investigating qualitative aspects of public-private partnerships, precisely because these concepts are not quantifiable. Success and failure in public policy are complicated, multi-dimensional concepts (McConnell 2010) that necessarily include some highly subjective components. Success, in particular, is difficult to measure in a democracy, because success for some groups often implies failure for others. Evaluations of success can be quite meaningless unless they specify success for whom (Newman 2014; Newman and Head 2015).

Failure, while still subjective, can be easier to determine in part because policy failure can be a failure for everyone, as exemplified by the United Kingdom's experience with bovine spongiform encephalopathy, otherwise known as "mad cow" disease (Van Zwanenberg and Millstone 2003). Moreover, the consequences of failures in public policy are often more palpable than the benefits of successes, because people experience sickness, loss of human life, and dispossession of property more sharply than they feel saved from something that has been prevented from happening. Policy failures can become outright disasters, in which people's lives and livelihoods are affected dramatically, as was seen in the recovery efforts in the southern US states after Hurricane Katrina (Birkland and Waterman 2008). In contrast, policy successes like universal health care or crime reduction will have more subtle benefits that are only apparent in the long term. In addition, punishments to political actors resulting from policy failures are often stronger than the rewards they might accrue from policy success (Newman and Bird 2017). Consequently, as McConnell (2010) has observed, policy failure has been much more widely studied than policy success.

This focus on failure is paralleled in other areas. For example, a vast literature has arisen on the subject of market failures, discussing their existence or non-existence, debating the need to correct them or not, and defining the consequences of government intervention in what might otherwise be activities of actors within the private market – but "market success" is a concept that is not as frequently investigated. Likewise, government failure, in which government intervention can result in a failure to achieve its own goals (see Wolf 1987 for example), gathers more attention than government success.

Since public-private partnerships are, by definition, collaborations between governments and non-government entities, the focus in this book will be on the successes and failures of governance arrangements that can be achieved when public and private sector actors work together to pursue social goals. Now more than ever, governments and non-government entities must collaborate to deliver public programming (Goodwin 1998, 5–6; Stoker 1998, 19–22; Jessop 2000, 16–18; Aikins 2009, 406). In this new paradigm of governance, the consequences of the use of collaborative policy instruments like P3s, such as influences on democratic accountability and on the ability to achieve public policy goals, are still unclear. Jessop (1998, 43) argues that systems of governance, like markets or governments alone, are prone to failure – but governance failures have so far received little attention (see Dixon and Dogan 2002 for an early attempt at a theoretical approach to governance failure). This represents a significant gap in the collective knowledge about governance arrangements, especially since collaborative efforts such as P3s are increasingly seen as effective methods of developing infrastructure and delivering public services (Garvin and Bosso 2008, 162; Siemiatycki 2010, 43).

In order to gain a full understanding of the role of the state in governing P3s, it will therefore be necessary to delve into concepts of governance failure, in which governments and private companies cannot sustain collaborative arrangements for mutually beneficial outcomes. Just like in the analogous literatures discussed above, it will be more challenging to identify governance success than governance failure, because success requires more specific subjective interpretations than failure, and its consequences are more subtle and less immediately apparent. For these reasons, I will place more emphasis on factors that can help prevent governance failure than on those that can contribute to governance success – although both will be discussed.

STUDYING TRANSPORTATION

Transportation (especially, but not exclusively, public transit) has frequently been included in inventories of public services (see Le Grand 1987; Galambos and Baumol 2000, 305; Winston 2000, 404) and has been described as a target of government intervention (Jones 1984; Rephann 1993; Rietveld and Stough 2007, 1). Transportation has been associated with state-building (Jones 1984; Perl 1994), and railways, highways, inland canals, ferry services, and airlines have historically been of interest to national and sub-national governments. Although the marketization of transportation may not be a new phenomenon in some countries (see Perl and Newman 2012 for example), because of its historical ties to government action, it is a good area in which to study the impact of increasing the participation of the private sector in the delivery of public services. In many countries, the use of P3 arrangements for transportation infrastructure increased substantially throughout the 1990s and early 2000s (Levinson et al. 2007, 301–2).

But more specifically, transportation constitutes a prime venue for analyzing the impact of P3s on the attainment of public policy objectives. Because transportation projects usually involve the construction of large pieces of infrastructure (such as highways, ports, airports, and subway systems), they are invariably associated with enormous capital expenses and long-term, detailed, and costly maintenance plans. In order to entice participants from the private sector into engaging in a partnership that will be expensive and will demand long-term commitment, a transportation P3 contract will often require a partnership agreement that lasts at least 25 years, so that the private partner can be assured of an appropriate return on investment. Long-term commitment is especially necessary if the private sector partner is to be repaid by collecting user fees or tolls, because the unpredictability of patronage imposes an added risk to the project and to the partnership. This risk would not be present in other policy areas where it is not possible to charge the user directly – such as wastewater management, for example, in which activities like rain water run-off and public sewer drainage are not directly attributable to individual customers. P3 projects in those other industries would be exposed to much less risk because they would be funded by government repayment mechanisms, which are more reliable than revenue generated by user fees.

In spite of the potential for collecting user fees (or perhaps, because of the unpredictable nature of this form of repayment), transportation P3s also often contain contractual stipulations of revenue guarantees. Lengthy concession periods, revenue guarantees, and shared revenue streams are all factors that generate controversy in P3 contracts (Hodge and Bowman 2004). In other words, P3 arrangements in transportation present an arena in which several of the most contentious aspects of public-private partnership contracts are frequently used together. In addition, transportation P3s also entail the kinds of controversies that are endemic to P3s in most other policy areas, such as sealed contracts, secrecy of contract negotiations, and unfortunate financial arrangements involving "tax leakage," in which ongoing public sector costs at one level of government are inflated by the taxes that private sector P3 partners must pay to other levels of government (Poschmann 2003).

Moreover, transportation P3s present some of the best examples for study, because there is less scope for variation in the partnership arrangement than there is in other policy areas. With hospitals or prisons, the diversity of tasks involved in their operations (doctors, laboratories, cafeterias, prison guards, administration, etc.) allows for a much wider variety of sub-divided P3 arrangements, which means P3s can be used for smaller sub-components of operation and could thereby avoid potential conflicts (see Grimsey and Lewis 2004, 96–102, for a detailed discussion of various P3 options for hospitals and prisons). While transportation infrastructure may require multiple processes for design and construction, in operation it will require its many functions to be integrated for the single task of enabling objects and people to move from one location to another. The unity of operations for transportation, combined with the potential for direct access to revenue supplied by the user mentioned above, could expose transportation P3s to potential governance conflicts that projects in other policy areas are currently able to avoid.

However, the kinds of contractual obligations to the private sector partner that are popular in transportation P3s have been and continue to be used in other areas (the contract for the province of Alberta's Special Waste Management System P3, in operation from 1986 to 1995, for example, contained revenue guarantees. See Boardman et al. 2005, 178). As P3s become more popular and political confidence in them grows – and as advances in technology continue to develop – long contracts, revenue guarantees, and user fees could all be employed in a wider variety of P3 projects, and more often. My findings from transportation will illuminate aspects of P3 arrangements that are currently used in part – but could soon be used in whole – in many other areas of service delivery.

Although a number of authors have speculated as to how these common contractual elements of P3s – and especially, the conflict they can potentially enable – might affect the achievement of public policy goals (see Langford 1999; Greve and Hodge 2010, for example), the effect of public-private partnerships on public service delivery is a relatively unexplored domain. As transportation P3s represent a logical extreme in P3 arrangements, it is reasonable to begin the research there and to work toward the middle as the research agenda matures.

COMPARING THE CASES

The two cases that I have chosen, the Canada Line and the Sydney Airport Link, represent a unique opportunity to compare nearly identical P3 projects that resulted in dramatically different outcomes. The two cases share many characteristics. Both involve rail extensions of metropolitan public transit networks. Both connect the downtown core of a major metropolis with an international airport and continue on to the suburbs. Both are infrastructure projects that required hundreds of millions of dollars in capital investment. And both involved extensive tunnelling under urban centres, including the use of complicated and expensive tunnel boring techniques. Moreover, the Canada Line and the Sydney Airport Link were each projects driven by sub-national governments in a federal system (i.e., British Columbia and New South Wales, respectively). Each case was structured as a public-private partnership with substantial capital investment from the private sector. Each involved private ownership of assets, fixed-price design-build construction contracts, private sector operations and maintenance, and thirty-five-year concession periods. And finally, each was built in anticipation of an Olympiad and faced similar political motivation and pressures surrounding the Olympics bid and the event itself.

However, while the Canada Line could be seen as a success (it has exceeded ridership expectations by a wide margin and continues to increase patronage), the Sydney Airport Link debuted at around one-quarter of expected patronage, and after five years of service, a financial restructuring, and a revised P3 contract, only saw negligible improvement in patronage levels (Nixon 2006). Moreover, while the Canada Line has successfully deflected more than one major lawsuit, the Sydney Airport Link has suffered from legal action between the public and private sector partners, the bankruptcy of the original private sector consortium, and a renegotiated revenue-sharing arrangement that resulted in an increased cost to the public sector of about $151 million.[3]

Canada and Australia are, of course, very similar political jurisdictions in that they are both federated Westminster parliamentary governments with, excluding the province of Quebec, legal traditions based on common law precedents. Both Canada and Australia are (majority) English-speaking countries with historical colonial ties to Great Britain and comparable themes of the legacy

3 All currency is in 2014 Canadian dollars unless otherwise stated. My calculations use the Consumer Price Index from the Australian Bureau of Statistics and Statistics Canada, and annual exchange rates from the Bank of Canada. All dollar figures are meant to be approximate.

of interaction with indigenous populations. These countries have similar economic dependencies on natural resource extraction and are reacting to the same global economic forces such as a realignment in international commodities markets. Moreover, comparing Canada and Australia is a tradition that goes back several decades (see Albinski 1973 for example). This high level of similarity at the contextual level enhances the most similar systems case study approach used here, because not only are the cases themselves as alike as possible but the national, political, and jurisdictional settings under which they exist are also very aligned. Thus, any difference in outcomes is not likely to be attributable to issues of unique national context.

The Canada Line and the Sydney Airport Link are therefore nearly perfect candidates for a comparison of success and failure in public-private partnerships. In my analysis, I rely mainly on three methods of data collection: elite interviews, primary document analysis, and published secondary source literature. I conducted semi-structured interviews with twenty-four individuals, including former and current CEOs and other executives from the private sector partners in both cases, one former premier, two former transportation ministers, several high-ranking executives from relevant public sector agencies and from the airport authorities in both cases, a former city councillor, multiple civil servants at the state/provincial and municipal levels, and one prominent transportation activist. Anonymity was promised to all interview subjects, which resulted in remarkably candid, cooperative, and enthusiastic responses. Each of these interviews provided a wealth of information, both factual and interpretive, that provides considerable consistency when held against a backdrop of multiple other interview responses and published documents.

In the chapters that follow, I will analyze these two cases to show that actions taken by the government and other public sector agencies contributed to success and helped to prevent governance failure in the Canada Line P3, whereas the absence of these factors produced the opposite results in the Sydney Airport Link P3. Contrary to the position held by most proponents of P3s, who tend to emphasize the benefits of the market side of P3s while ignoring the importance of the public sector, active policy leadership on the part of the state contributed to the successful outcomes in the Vancouver case while its absence contributed to failure in the Sydney case. In fact, allowing the private partner too much free reign in a public-private partnership is a recipe for governance failure, as the Sydney case will clearly illustrate.

2

Public-Private Partnerships

Private sector firms and public sector organizations can collaborate to deliver services to the public, but why should they? Private firms and governments do not usually have the same objectives, so it is logical that they might also perform different functions in the economy and in society. Are there goods that should be provided solely by the private market, and others entirely by the state? And how can we tell the difference?

In reality, of course, there is a lot of interaction between the public and private sectors, and provision purely by one or the other is unusual. Public and private entities can compete in the same arena, as they sometimes do in municipal garbage collection; they can operate in parallel, performing similar functions for different populations, as they might do for health care; and they can collaborate in a variety of mixed enterprise modes, as they do in transportation. In theory, the nature of the goods or service being provided should help explain the likely configuration of public and private sector interaction. However, social values, political objectives, and ideologies can inspire some more creative service delivery arrangements.

THEORETICAL PERSPECTIVES
ON THE PROVISION OF GOODS AND SERVICES

Many scholars who are interested in the material aspects of public service delivery (see, for example, Savas 2000; Batley 2001; Moaven-zadeh and Markow 2007) divide goods and services along two separate lines: excludability and competitiveness. Goods and services that are excludable are those that some customers or recipients can be prevented from accessing. Goods and services that are competitive are those that are in limited supply and so if one customer or recipient is using it, another may not be able to. There are four different possibilities for goods and services in this model (see Figure 2.1):

1 Private Consumer Goods (excludable and competitive): all private goods, like televisions, appliances, homes, cars. Exclusion is usually achieved through pricing. Competition is dealt with through supply and demand.
2 Large-scale Services (excludable and non-competitive): most utilities, like drinking water or electricity, and large-scale services like insurance or internet access. Exclusion is achieved in this case by charging customers for service and denying access to non-payers.
3 Public Space (non-excludable and competitive): e.g., public roads. Without a toll system, roads can be accessed by anyone. However, not all cars can use a single road at the same time, as this will result in traffic congestion.
4 Public Goods (non-excludable and non-competitive): a number of services are delivered in a way that makes it difficult to charge customers directly, and can also be used by all customers at once. Examples are national defence, police forces, fire protection, and snow removal.

Since customers cannot be prevented from using a non-excludable service, it is difficult in those cases to charge users directly for use. Private companies in a free-market economy are motivated by profit; therefore, it stands to reason that they would not have much interest in non-excludable goods and services. Accordingly, the only way to fund these services is through coerced payment (i.e., taxes) or through voluntary contributions (Savas 2000, 53). In this respect, it is often argued that for non-excludable goods and services, and especially for public goods, collective (i.e., government) provision is the most logical and efficient method of delivery (Moavenzadeh and Markow 2007, 132).

Transportation infrastructure can be excludable, as in rail transit with fare gates that control access, or non-excludable, as is common with ordinary city roads in which it is difficult to charge dri-

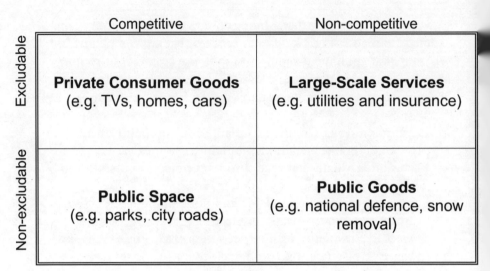

Figure 2.1 Excludability and competitiveness of goods and services

vers the exact cost of their use. Infrastructure projects in general, as well as many public utilities, are often excludable but require economies of scale and enormous capital investments to be economically efficient. In these scenarios, usually termed "natural monopolies," a single provider is more efficient than a competitive market because high capital costs and technical obstacles (like establishing a dedicated right-of-way for a rail line through a busy urban center) create barriers of entry for firms wanting to compete in the marketplace. Even though natural monopolies can be excludable, in any particular natural monopoly situation there may be no private firms willing to take on the risk and cost of setting up operations. In these cases, as in cases of non-excludable goods, a particular policy objective may require public investment because the market may be unable to fulfill it alone.

Both of the cases considered in this book are examples of natural monopolies, not standard consumer goods as would be implied by their status as excludable and competitive services. In both scenarios, the private sector demonstrated a documented unwillingness to meet the initial requirements of the scope and scale of the projects. In fact, although the Sydney case was initially conceived as being entirely funded by the private sector, this financial model was quickly abandoned as it became clear that the private sector partners were unwilling or unable to provide the more than $1 billion that the project would eventually cost (Coultan 1994). In Vancouver, the final and winning bid from the private sector still fell short of the expected private sector funding, and resulted in an adjustment to the funding provided by the public sector partners (Cohn 2008, 35). In both examples, as is generally the case with natural monopolies, the public sector's input was required to help bring the project to reality, as the free market would not produce the service on its own.

However, public goods and natural monopolies are not the only situations in which the lines between markets and governments can be crossed. Private firms in a competitive market will not spontaneously fulfill the government's social and political objectives, such as state-building, national unity, redistribution of resources, or the economic development of a particular industry or region. Of course, government action in support of these goals is often framed as a prevention or correction of a perceived failure of the market. For example, in both the Canada Line and Sydney Airport Link cases, urban development was cited as a rationale for building the rail line (New South Wales 1994; RAV Project Management Ltd. 2003, 12), implying that public intervention was required to promote residential and commercial property improvement in neighbourhoods that would not have experienced development under ordinary market conditions.

In actual practice, although there are theoretical prescriptions for which kinds of goods and services ought to be provided by the private market and which ought to be provided by the state, the public and private sectors do not operate along clearly defined boundaries at all. Governments depend on private companies to provide labour, capital investment, technical experience, and innovation even when social and political objectives are of primary importance. In more recent times, negative images of "big government," an aversion to public debt and deficit spending, and perceptions of excessive red tape and public sector waste have inspired governments to hire private corporations to deliver public services even when market conditions are theoretically unfavourable for the private sector. This can result in various arrangements such as contracting out services, outsourcing labour, subsidizing or guaranteeing private investment, and a wide range of other alternative service delivery mechanisms.

More accurately, then, there is a continuum of public and private involvement in society and in the economy, ranging from purely private market delivery to pure government provision (Savas 2000, 241). In the space between these extremes lie all forms of public sector/ private sector collaboration, including public-private partnerships.

PUBLIC-PRIVATE PARTNERSHIPS: DEFINITIONS AND KEY ISSUES

There is some disagreement as to what exactly is meant by the term "public-private partnership" (de Bettignies and Ross 2004, 136). For instance, Bult-Spiering and Dewulf (2006, 16–19) and Allan (2001, 6–8) list many definitions of P3s given by numerous authors, but each one is slightly different than the next, with no general consensus on a precise definition. An additional confounding layer is provided by Dunn (2000, 77–8), who makes the distinction between "policy-level partnerships," in which private sector delivery of a service may be subject to government regulation, and "project-based partnerships," in which the public and private sectors collaborate on the service's actual construction or delivery. Koppenjan and Enserink (2009, 285–6) further divide P3s into three separate categories (operations/maintenance /service, build/operate/invest, and joint ventures) according to the level of involvement of the private sector. The state of the academic literature seems to suggest that every author must begin a discussion of P3s by attempting to create a novel definition of the phenomenon.

This difficulty in establishing a precise definition is a result of the fact that P3s represent a variety of collaborative activities, rather than one particular mechanism. I consider Hodge and Bowman's definition of P3s as "a family of integrated partnership modes by which asset and service provision may be supplied to the public sector" (2004, 203) to be the most useful. This definition acknowledges that P3s constitute a spectrum of activities and arrangements rather than one specific mode. In addition, the Hodge and Bowman definition states unequivocally that P3s refer to private sector involvement in areas of public service delivery that have previously been considered the domain of the public sector. This definition is flexible enough to account for different configurations of P3 arrangements, yet it still frames the discussion on P3s as a means through which to include the private sector in public sector activity.

It is possible, however, to build on this definition in order to gain greater precision. Contractual public-private partnerships are distinguishable from other forms of interaction between the public and private sectors, and in particular, there are two elements that are necessarily common to all P3s in theory and in practice. First, the word "partnership" in the term "public-private partnership" implies, at the very least, a sharing of risks, responsibilities, or rewards (Allan 2001). For this reason, when a government hires a private company to deliver a service on the government's terms (often referred to as "contracting out"), this should not be considered a P3. In these instances, the private contractor does not share in the risks or responsibilities of providing the service to the public, and there is no shared revenue as the contractor is paid a fixed amount that is stipulated in advance (Grimsey and Lewis 2004, 57). Under this arrangement, the government is still the supplier and provider of the service to the public, and the contractor is merely used as a mechanism for delivery. Likewise, a situation in which a private company hires a public agency to perform a specific task – as the private operator of Ontario's 407 ETR toll highway does when it pays the Ontario Provincial Police to patrol traffic violations on the highway – is again not a P3, because the public sector police force is merely a contracted agent and not a partner with decision-making responsibility. And finally, a complete divestiture of a public property or agency to a private firm – often referred to as "privatization" – is not a P3 either, because in these instances the public sector has relinquished its responsibility for delivering that service to the public, and the private firm takes on all risks, responsibilities, and rewards attached to service delivery in that area. While many different varieties of P3 exist in practice today (see Grimsey and Lewis 2004, 54, for a list of various P3 configurations), any true P3 would necessarily involve some shared level of capital investment, cooperative responsibility for decision making, or shared revenue stream between the public and private sector partners.

Second, in all P3s, the sharing of investment, responsibility, risks, or rewards (or some combination thereof) is governed by a contract that is legally binding on both the private and public sector partners. These contracts are the defining documents of the partnership: they specify the nature of the partnership and the tasks demanded of the partners, they delineate the allocation of responsibilities and risks, and they provide for dispute resolution mechanisms. P3 contracts are ultimately adjudicated by courts, not by legislatures, and they are often sealed from public view as they are private arrangements that can sometimes be shielded from Freedom of Information laws. All of the above elements are seen in the contracts for both the Canada Line and the Sydney Airport Link.

Because of their formulation as a legal partnership between independent agents, P3s are effectively a method of implementing public policy via contract rather than through legislation (Grimsey and Lewis 2004). It is this use of binding partnership contracts in the implementation of public policy that makes the P3 arrangement so unique. A contractual partnership arrangement for the delivery of public programming is different from other forms of public goods or service delivery (including conventional public delivery, government subsidy of private enterprise, and state-owned enterprise), in that the partnership contract attains legal superiority over other government instruments. While governments can (in principle) rescind or amend laws as they see fit, they cannot easily abrogate a contract with a private entity. Just as Western mixed economies depend on private actors to fulfill important societal and economic functions, these private entities act on the assumption that their contracts are safe and will be enforced. Widespread abrogation of contracts "would decrease the willingness of private parties to enter into agreements with local governments" (Griffith 1990, 283; for a more detailed discussion of the above argument, see Hodge and Bowman 2004).

This precedence of contracts over statutes creates the potential for conflict. Since P3 contracts are adjudicated by the courts and not by legislatures, and since many P3s have long contract periods as described above, it is very realistic that future governments might be bound by contractual obligations that could constrain their ability to implement their chosen policies. For example, between 2003 and 2006, the government of the Canadian province of Ontario attempted to fulfill an election promise of reducing tolls on the privately operated Highway 407, but it was prevented from doing so by a successful legal action in which the highway's concessionaire rightfully claimed that they were the sole authority on pricing the highway's tolls, as was specified in their contract (Campbell 2006). This has implications for our understanding of the democratic state, in which elected politicians are expected to be able to enact and enforce policy on behalf of the population they represent. In the Highway 407 example, policy alternatives that would have been compatible with the P3 contract, such as subsidizing the tolls with public funding, would have been a risky political move – as evidenced by the repercussions of a similar measure taken by the government of New Brunswick three years earlier (McHardie 2011). In any case, since the private sector concessionaire had full legal rights to set the tolls on the highway, they could not be compelled to lower the fees even through subsidization. The government would have had to refund money directly to users, a costly and highly ambitious endeavour.

Long-term contracts between the public and private sector, as seen with infrastructure P3s, can be sources of other kinds of conflict as well. As it is impossible to make predictions about the distant future, no P3 contract will ever perfectly account for all of the financial, business cycle, technological, and political changes that may arise over the length of the concession period (Hodge and Bowman 2004). This phenomenon, known as the principle of incomplete contracts (Cruz and Marques 2013; Hart 2003), frequently results in the renegotiation of contracts before their original end dates – as often as 75 per cent of the time in some industries and 55 per cent of the time for transportation projects in some countries (Marques and Berg 2010, 335). It would be very tidy to design and negotiate a perfect P3 contract, and then set the project in motion and allow it to govern itself. In reality, even the best contracts are open to ambiguity and vulnerable to events that are beyond the ability of contract designers to forecast. Ongoing positive interaction between the public and private partners is required throughout the life of the concession, because no contract can account for all possibilities over a multi-decade concession period. Unforeseen circumstances will inevitably produce conflict.

Consider, for instance, a P3 service in which variations in demand cause extreme fluctuations in profitability. In theory, this kind of risk ought to be calculated, priced, and divided appropriately between the partners, so that each partner takes on the risk that they are best able to handle. Risk transfer is often cited as one of the major benefits of using a P3 arrangement for infrastructure over pure public sector provision (Ball 2011, 11; Yescombe 2007, 18). In general, construction risk is usually assumed by the private sector partner, so that budgetary setbacks and cost overruns due to scheduling delays do not fall to the public purse. The public sector partner might then assume some of the demand risk by applying a minimum revenue guarantee for the private investors. In a P3, at least some components of construction risk and operations risk are usually "bundled" to motivate the private partner to spread appropriate resources across multiple aspects of production and delivery (de Bettignies and Ross 2004).

In practice, partners in a P3 are often surprised by demand variation (Engel et al. 2013, 84), and conflict can ensue as blame is passed around and the partners seek to extract damages from each other. This is precisely what happened to the Sydney Airport Link P3: demand was significantly lower than predicted by the preliminary estimates, which resulted in the bankruptcy of the private sector partner. This led to a legal dispute between the partners in which the private investors sued the government for damages, alleging that the government had not lived up to its end of the agreement. In the end, the contract was renegotiated in a way that disadvantaged the government by reducing its share of revenue. In this case, although the demand risk was supposed to be held by the private partner (who had full authority in setting user fees), the design of the contract and the uncertainty of demand for the service led to incomplete risk transfer that was not predicted by the contract's original negotiators.

In truth, the capacity of P3s as a mechanism for transferring risk is a subject of much controversy. While some argue that the transfer of risks away from the state is one of the primary reasons for engaging in public-private partnerships (Asenova and Beck 2003; Nisar 2007), others have been more critical (Flinders 2005; Quiggin 2004; Siemiatycki and Farooqi 2012). Critics mainly argue that private companies and investors engaging in P3s will charge excess premiums to take on risk, or that the true cost of risks to the public sector may not be known or may be hidden within overall project costs (Coulson 2008; Hodge 2004). Critics further argue that risk is never fully transferred to the private sector, because the private partner is always a special-purpose vehicle that can go bankrupt if necessary to avoid responsibility (Quiggin 2005, 447). In any case, governments seek to fulfill social and political objectives. If a private partner were to go bankrupt or otherwise withdraw while financing a P3 project, the state would presumably still want to complete the project in order to achieve its policy goals. This is what happened when the private partner withdrew from the London Underground improvement and maintenance P3 in 2007 – the UK Department of Transport assumed the costs and continued with the project (Milmo 2009). And lastly, governments take on considerable political risks when engaging in public-private ventures – risks that cannot be transferred to the private sector, because in the event that outcomes are negative, there is always the chance that voters will associate the government with the failure of the project, even if the private partner assumes responsibility for failure (Rufín and Rivera-Santos 2012, 1639–40).

Other reasons for engaging in P3s are also contentious. In appeals for public support for P3 projects, political actors often claim that the P3 format will allow them to access private capital for investment in public infrastructure or service delivery. This argument was used by governments in support of P3s for both the Canada Line and the Airport Link projects (e.g., Baird 1992b, 8101; Bridge 2003). In some jurisdictions – notably in developing countries – partnership with the private sector may very well be a good way to access the capital required for investment in infrastructure (see for example, Gerhager and Sahooly 2009). However, this rationale for industrialized countries is doubted by most analysts, including experts from different ideological perspectives (e.g., Poschmann 2003, 3; Vining and Boardman 2008; Sawyer 2009, 50–1). For one thing, private capital investment must be repaid, with a suitable rate of return. These repayments are financed either through tax revenue, in which case the benefit of private capital is neutralized, or through user fees, which do not enhance the government's financial position (Engel et al. 2013) because they represent a lost opportunity on the part of the government to charge its own user fees (Daniels and Trebilcock 2000).[1] The decision to use private finance may more realistically be based on a desire to "reduce government spending and limit government's role in the economy" (Moavenzadeh and Markow 2007, 130).

There are more material reasons to engage in public-private partnerships. For the private sector, P3s represent profitable revenue streams that were not previously available on the private market. Governments, on the other hand, may choose to collaborate with private corporations in order to gain from the technical experience or from the existing enterprise of a private firm already involved in a particular industry, or to capitalize on perceived efficiencies in the private sector that would hopefully lead to lower costs, better choices for citizens, or improved technology.

On this last point, many scholars agree that private sector efficiencies are most apparent in a P3 when it can harness the classic advantage of the free market: competition (Hakim et al. 1996; Rosenau 2000; Batley 2001). In theory, in a competitive environment, firms will seek to improve technology, reduce costs, provide more and better choices to customers, and deliver projects faster than a single provider – government or private sector –

1　There is an ongoing and highly charged debate on the way that financing in public-private partnerships should be evaluated. The main points of contention involve the Public Sector Comparator, which is the dominant method of comparing P3 procurement with traditional public provision, and the discount rates used to measure the cost of public and private borrowing. This debate is not critical to the present discussion, but I would point the interested reader to Quiggin (2004) and Burgess and Jenkins (2010) for opposing viewpoints on this matter.

could hope to do in a monopoly environment. This is most easily accomplished when the service in question is excludable and competitive, according to the typology discussed earlier (Moavenzadeh and Markow 2007). However, as explained above, P3s are often used to attract private sector involvement in areas that are non-excludable or non-competitive, such as water treatment, hospitals, prisons, highways, and public transportation. In these instances, competition among private sector firms is limited to the procurement phase of the project, in which multiple firms will bid for the P3 partnership. Once the contract is signed, only a single firm (often, a consortium of several distinct corporations cooperating through a jointly owned special purpose vehicle) will hold the P3 concession for the life of the contract. Presumably, at the end of the contract, the concessionaire will have to compete for the right to renew the contract for another concession period (although given the current youthfulness of most P3s, this form of competition has yet to be tested widely). Competition in P3s is therefore longitudinal rather than cross-sectional: firms compete in isolated, serial contests spaced apart by multiple decades, but winners are awarded contracts that are essentially competition-free for substantial periods of time. Therefore, the benefits of market competition for P3s may not be as straight-forward as traditional economic theory – which is based on ongoing, nearly continuous competition for streams of customers – might suggest.

Ultimately, all statements in favour of using public-private partnerships for public service delivery hinge on the argument that the state acting alone will not deliver the best possible service to the public. Different perspectives will take diverging normative positions on the overall desirability, and the optimal extent, of the removal of the public sector from service delivery, but in general, the debates on economic issues and contract arrangements presented above are all based on this central principle. P3s are designed to remove some – but not all – elements of the state and replace them with some – but not all – aspects of the private sector.

At its very core, this is what public-private partnership is about. In many countries, especially in the US and Europe, P3s have been associated with a decreased role and responsibility for government and an attendant increased use of private capital (Dewulf et al. 2012, 3). One of the primary reasons for engaging in a P3 is to allow "a reduction in the size of a public agency by substituting private-sector resources and personnel" (Levy 2011, 7). P3s are seen, by authors on all sides of the political spectrum, as being linked to privatization; they are meant to enable "a roll-back of the state" in order to extend the "benefits of privatisation to core public services which could not be privatised" (Yescombe 2007, 16). P3s are part of a philosophy that believes that the role of the state is to formulate policy, but that implementation should be left to the private sector (Falch and Henten 2010, 497). This is often justified by reference to a slow, bureaucratic, inefficient, and ineffective public sector, where "there is a long history of publicly procured contracts being delayed and turning out to be more expensive than budgeted" (Grimsey and Lewis 2005, 346). In fact, all of the benefits of P3s that have been described rely on the removal of the public sector from service delivery: the efficiency of the private sector, the potential for innovation generated through market competition, and the transfer of risk away from the public purse, for example, all imply that P3s are effective when the state retreats from service delivery in favour of the private market.

This philosophy is emphasized by proponents of P3s, and for many authors the key to success in public-private partnerships is to increase the freedom allotted to the private sector in decision making and in the general implementation of public service delivery. In analyzing P3s in the United States, Papajohn et al. argue that administration in a P3 should be handled by the private sector "to avoid some of the overly complex government procedures and political influences and thus expedite the process of project delivery" (2011, 130). Other authors cite the "capricious nature of the public sector" as well as its other "deficiencies ... such as ineffective policy and strategy, non-professional project origination and identification," all of which "can lead to problems in PPPs including poor procurement incentives, lack of coordination and high transaction costs" (Yuan et al. 2009, 254). P3s must be protected from excessive government intervention through an administrative buffer, "as government objectives for political or social reasons may act as a disincentive to investment" (Pongsiri 2002, 490). Governments, according to some, ought to remove themselves from asset management and instead concentrate on regulation and oversight (TD Bank Financial Group 2006).

However, the difference between public-private partnerships and privatization is that in a P3, the state is expected to retain a role – albeit one of oversight rather than direct action. Public sector involvement is often justified as being required to ensure accountability, to protect vulnerable segments of the public, and to reduce the impact of negative externalities, such as pollution, inequitable distribution of public services, or reduction in service quality in the name of profit (Rosenau 2000; Dewulf et al. 2012, 29). As mentioned in the previous chapter, this creates something of a paradox, as one of the supposed benefits of using a P3 is to replace the inefficient bureaucracy of government with the efficiency of the private sector, but another supposed benefit is the control of negative externalities and the promotion of transparency through public sector accountability (Grimsey and Lewis 2004, 17). In other words, the point of using a public-private partnership rather than direct government provision is to keep the government out, because the private sector is supposedly more efficient; however, the point of using a public-private partnership rather than complete privatization is to keep the government in, so as to ensure accountability.

P3s remain controversial policy instruments. Even their acceptance by governments and by the general public is a source of debate, with some scholars arguing that they are gaining in popularity with governments (Coghill and Woodward 2005), others claiming public sector resistance (Faulkner 2004, 66–7), and still others suggesting that the general public itself may be "deeply sceptical about, and even hostile to" P3s (Grimsey and Lewis 2004, 17). While P3s do not aim to remove benefits or reduce social programming, they do frequently transfer decision making from the state to the private sector, and citizens who are accustomed to modern welfare state principles may therefore be suspicious of public-private partnership and its potential effects on social welfare services (Grimsey and Lewis 2004, 17; United Nations 2008, 59). Vote-conscious governments will have to take this into consideration.

HISTORICAL CONTEXT
AND THE PRESENT RESEARCH AGENDA

Despite the existence of controversy, P3s do not constitute a radical redirection in public policy. Rather, public-private cooperation has existed for centuries. For a long time, roads and bridges were maintained by private individuals on behalf of the state, under an arrangement of shared revenue. The revenue stream (in the form of tolls) was as important then as it is in modern P3s, as this was the incentive for the private partner to enter into the agreement (Lockwood 2007). In France, public-private collaboration was instrumental in creating a national rail network (Jones 1984). And in a more precise example, Grimsey and Lewis (2004) describe a situation in eighteenth-century England in which a private investor was provided a concession to build and maintain lighthouses for a set period of time, during which he was provided with a share of the docking fees of the local ports. In a striking parallel to modern P3s, the English government at the time contended that not enough public funds were available to build all of the lighthouses needed on this particular stretch of coast.

However, public-private partnership experienced a decline throughout the bulk of the twentieth century, when direct market intervention through regulation and state-owned enterprise became more popular forms of economic management. This was the heyday of the welfare state, in which many governments took on a vastly increased capacity to deliver a minimum universal level of public services in many areas (such as health, higher education, family planning, research and development, pollution control, and so on) and intervened in industrial markets in various sectors. The development of the welfare state was connected with what Esping-Andersen (1999, 7–8) calls "the egalitarian agenda": a deliberate attempt to create an individual-centered, rights-based social benefits program, in which class issues involving the income mobility of lower wage earners were made less relevant by the institution of universal social rights. This program (in conjunction with a general rise in prosperity related to the abundance of secure, low-skill, high-wage, manufacturing jobs) was so successful, that as it evolved it became self-perpetuating: empowered working classes merged with middle classes and demanded ever-increasing social rights (Esping-Andersen 1999, 15). This resulted in a substantial decrease in private sector activity in areas of social programming, and public-private partnership as it had previously been known became at most a marginal occurrence in many countries.

After the energy crises in the 1970s and the trend toward neoliberal politics in the 1980s, however, the use of contractual partnership relationships as a policy instrument for public service delivery reappeared in many jurisdictions. P3s are now seen as a way to deliver services, programming, and infrastructure without dramatically increasing the public budget or necessitating a rise in taxes (Levinson et al. 2007). Many scholars have remarked that P3s have recently exploded in numbers (Teisman and Klijn 2002; Garvin and Bosso 2008; Siemiatycki 2010), especially since the UK pioneered the Private Finance Initiative in the 1990s (de Bettignies and Ross 2004).[2] In the last 20 years, P3s have appeared in the Netherlands (Klijn and Teisman 2004), Canada (Siemiatycki 2006), the US (Boardman et al. 2005), Sweden (Almqvist and Högberg 2005), New Zealand (Cervin 2000), Germany (Oppen et al. 2005), and Australia (Harding 2001), among many other places. P3s have emerged in a wide variety of areas, including public transit, hospitals, schools, and prisons.

The modern increased use of P3s gives the subject a renewed relevance that demands scholarly attention. For one thing, the current political climate is dramatically different from the last period when public-private collaboration was popular. Before World War I, most developed countries operated under a laissez-faire style of economic and social management, with minimal state intervention in industry or the private market and limited social services. Many social services before the 1920s were delivered by private charities (Oakley 2006) and were available only to the extremely poor. In the twenty-first century, governments in most Western democracies now manage a wide range of social programs, from

2 The Private Finance Initiative is a specific program of public-private partnership that was developed in the United Kingdom in the early 1990s and continued through successive British governments after it was introduced. For a good discussion of it, see Dixon et al. 2006.

employment insurance to pensions to public transit to health care, but the state is undergoing a reorientation to what might prove to be a post-welfare state mode of governance. P3s are useful governance tools in part because they harmonize well with the political culture embedded in many modern governments. However, their reintroduction into public service delivery during a period in which the roles and responsibilities of the state are being significantly redefined presents a new cluster of policy problems for the state and society to contend with.

There are a number of scholars who have begun to address the challenges that P3s may pose to the attainment of public policy goals. Most of this work has taken the form of well-developed hypothesizing: authors have written that actors in P3 arrangements will necessarily be less accountable to the public and will operate under less oversight than employees of government departments and agencies (Langford 1999); that the long contractual periods common to P3s may have unknown consequences for governance since there is no way that any contractual partner could foresee all possible events throughout the lifetime of the contract (Greve and Hodge 2010); and that there is the danger of partisanship being introduced into public service delivery since there is no requirement for private-sector employees to be politically neutral (Langford 1999). On this last point, many authors, including Weber (1948 [1921]), Hansen and Levine (1988), and Aucoin (1995), have written about the benefits of an anonymous, politically neutral bureaucracy.

There have also been some empirical studies of the effects of using P3s for public service delivery. In one study, Teisman and Klijn (2002) questioned the role of P3s as a form of network governance and, using a P3 project in the Netherlands as a case study, showed that the public sector's penchant for hierarchy and control may prevent it from using partnerships effectively for governance. In another, Greenaway et al. (2007) analyzed the development of the Norfolk and Norwich hospital P3 in the UK and found that the partnership arrangement and the national-level policy network that emerged from the project effectively obscured accountability and reduced the democratic potential of local representatives. However, empirical studies of this nature are few and far between.

CONCLUSION

More generally, the use of p3s raises questions about the state's appropriate role in public service delivery, especially now that governments around the world manage extensive systems of state-delivered goods and services. With the state now delegating much responsibility for service delivery, but with continuous public support for services, it is unclear how much the state should delegate and what its role might be in managing, steering, and governing the actors that are increasingly being called on to provide these services.

What is missing from the academic literature on this subject is a connection between theories of what the state should do, and empirical research on what has actually been occurring as governments contract with private companies to deliver goods and services to the public. In the next chapter, I will begin to address this gap in the literature by examining some theoretical models of governance. In subsequent chapters, I will use my two case studies as empirical evidence of how the state should involve itself in a p3 mode of service delivery, if it is interested in preventing governance failure.

3

Governance and the Role of the State

Modern public-private partnerships represent more than just the re-emergence of a mode of public service delivery that had fallen out of style during the peak years of the welfare state. More importantly, P3s exemplify the changes that have occurred as a result of the shift from government to governance that has been happening since at least the 1980s. In that time, public policy decision making and responsibility for many aspects of public service delivery have increasingly been delegated to non-government entities, including for-profit private companies. Public-private partnerships are an instrument that typifies this shift, as they allow private companies to finance, own, and operate services and infrastructure that would have been completely under state control in previous decades.

Although P3s may not be new, their reappearance in a modern context of retrenchment of the state from service delivery provokes a number of questions. For one, what if things go wrong? What are the consequences of failures in public-private partnerships? Are these consequences different than failures in purely public modes of service delivery? Are consequences of failure different now than they would have been when arrangements similar to modern P3s were used before the advent of the welfare state?

The role of the state in service delivery is still evolving. While few would question that the waves of privatization of state-owned enterprise and deregulation of industry represent a step away from state delivery of public services (Derthick and Quirk 1985; MacAvoy et al. 2012), there are still many unresolved questions about how much these changes have affected people's access to services (Hacker 2004; Hemerijck 2013). If public services have changed, and if P3s are playing a part in this change, it would be worthwhile to perform a deeper examination of the mechanisms and dynamics of governance in which public-private partnerships are involved.

In this chapter, I will explore success and failure in modern governance and the ways in which the factors that contribute to success and failure are related to P3s. I will theorize that, despite retrenchment of the state from public service delivery and the general reorganization of responsibility for service delivery that has been occurring in many countries in recent decades, the state still has a primary role to play in policy decision making and in providing services to its citizens. Specifically, I will argue that the state is an actor of critical importance in preventing the failure of governance arrangements for service delivery, and that this argument extends to services delivered through public-private partnerships.

THEORIES OF SUCCESS AND FAILURE

In chapter 1, I argued that success and failure were not perfect opposites. In particular, I noted that the consequences of failure were often perceived more tangibly than the consequences of success, that the political punishments that come with failure can be stronger than the political rewards associated with success, and that it was more likely that failure could be experienced by everyone at the same time.

The differences between success and failure run down to the fundamental, definitional level. Failure of any kind must be defined as the inability to attain a particular goal, and governance failure can also be defined in these terms. Since the goal of governance is to allow multiple public and private sector actors to share responsibility for the delivery of public goods and services, governance arrangements can be deemed to have failed when sustainable collaboration between public and private sector partners is no longer possible. But success in governance is more elusive, because of the requirement of specifying success for whom. Gov-

ernance arrangements that function as intended may not be failures, but they would only be successful for those people who benefit from them.

In light of these differences, scholars and practitioners might be
more interested in learning how failure in P3s can be prevented
than they would be in learning how to ensure success. This is precisely the model followed by analogous literatures in other areas of
public policy, including discussions on market failure, government
failure, state failure, and policy failure.

For example, welfare economists have provided a well-articulat-
ed account of market failure, but, as previously noted, "market success" is a term that is not used nearly as often. Bator (1958, 351)
famously defined market failure as "the failure of a more or less
idealized system of price-market institutions to sustain 'desirable'
activities or to estop 'undesirable' activities, where 'activities' include
both consumption and production," and where the idealized market is errorless, perfect, and Pareto-maximizing.[1] In other words,
the objective of the free market in a capitalist economy is to
achieve an economically efficient and Pareto-optimal allocation of
scarce resources among producer firms and consumer individuals.
This means that any time the market cannot achieve this position,
it has failed. When the market functions, it is business as usual, but
declarations of "success" would have to be qualified with explana-
tions of who benefits and who suffers.

Four main situations arise that are believed to result in market
failure. The first two, public goods and natural monopolies, were
discussed in the previous chapter. The third involves externalities,
such as pollution, which are consequences of a product sold in a
market but whose effects are not accounted for in the price paid by
the consumer. In the fourth scenario – markets with asymmetric
information – producers know more about their products than
consumers do, or consumers know more about their preferences
than manufacturers do, and so the equilibrium price of the market
does not accurately represent supply and demand (Weimer and
Vining 2011). In these cases, welfare economists argue that government intervention is required to correct the market failure,

1 The choice of "estop" rather than "stop" is deliberate and connotes an
effort to plug up or fill in a gap.

either to restore economic efficiency or to redistribute resources so as to achieve some desired social outcome.

The various conditions that lead to market failure all produce circumstances in which the efficiency of the market is obstructed: for public goods (for example, street lighting), the market alone will not produce the quantity of the good demanded (or it may not be produced at all), because firms lack the ability to charge consumers directly for the product. In situations of natural monopoly (such as electricity generation), private firms will over-charge for their product because the economy of scale required for the enterprise will result in monopoly production and will be subject to the abuses that monopolists are in a position to pursue. In markets with externalities (for example, water pollution as a by-product of a mining operation), firms will undercharge, be-cause the cost of the externality will not be accounted for in the price of the product. And for cases of information asymmetry (for example, health insurance, where customers know more about their intended usage than providers do), the price of the product may be inflated or understated, as the case may be, depending on whether consumers or producers have more information than their counterparts.

As distrust in government intervention became the prevailing attitude in the 1980s, an account of government failure was advanced to mirror the theory of market failure. This modern nar-rative, built on the earlier work of neoliberal economists such as Friedman (1962) and Buchanan (1975), describes how government failures occur when a particular government intrusion into the marketplace either fails to correct the market failure to which it is targeted, or worsens the situation by reducing the economic effi-ciency of the market (Wolf 1987, 53).

However, the conditions that lead to government failure are not fully agreed upon. Wolf (1987; 1988) posits four circumstances that lead to government failure: situations in which the costs of intervention are disconnected from the revenues used to pay for it; internal politics, including personal career ambitions of public officials and rent-seeking; externalities derived from government intervention; and differing definitions of "social desirability." Le Grand (1991) argues that Wolf's conditions do not explain all sit-uations of government failure: in addition to Wolf's four circumstances, direct provision of goods will also result in government failure because the public sector does not operate under the pressure of competition or bankruptcy; government subsidy will fail because it will obscure the natural price mechanism of the market and shift the equilibrium position to one that is not economically efficient; and regulation will result in government failure because governments cannot acquire the necessary information to make a precise calculation of what an efficient allocation of a service should be. Even in more recent years there is still some disagreement as to what a mature account of government failure should look like (see Wallis and Dollery 2002, for example). For this reason, theories of government failure are "neither as comprehensive nor as powerful as the theory of market failure" (Weimer and Vining 2011, 157).

As with market failure, accounts of government failure define failure as the inability to achieve an objective. However, the goals of government in a democracy are obviously more numerous than simple market intervention. More generally, states aim to balance the interests of variously identified groups in society (ethnic, religious, language-based, class, age, etc., and often in overlapping combinations) in order to achieve peace, justice, and economic stability; to protect citizens from financial and physical harm through the use of policing, civil and criminal penalties, and national defence; to maintain a national economy and its associated currency; to provide diplomatic functions with other countries or sub-national units; and a myriad of other objectives that depend on the political culture and prevailing attitudes and priorities of citizens in various countries. There exist theories of "state failure" that deal with failures of governments in these areas, including the conditions that lead to war, civil conflict, economic collapse, and anarchy (e.g., Migdal 1988). As with market failure and government failure, these theories of state failure are framed in terms of the failure of the state to accomplish the various goals described above.

Failures in public policy can similarly be defined in terms of the failure to achieve particular policy objectives. Kerr (1976) argues that policies can be considered failures when they cannot or do not achieve their stated objectives. McConnell (2010, 56) defines a failed policy as one that "does not achieve the goals that propo-

nents set out to achieve." Walsh (2006, 495) provides a similar definition: "Policy failure occurs when the decision makers responsible for initiating the consideration of and approving new policies
conclude that current policy is no longer achieving the political
and program goals they prefer." In all of these definitions, the non-
achievement of the initial goals of a public policy is the essential
element of failure.

DEFINING GOVERNANCE FAILURE

In the past, markets and governments were seen as ideological
opposites (Jessop 2000, 15). For all of the objectives of government intervention in the marketplace that were pursued during
the welfare state era, including correction of market failures, state-
building, and democratic egalitarianism, the market was seen
as the logical alternative. This is a reasonable assumption in advanced democracies, where market mechanisms historically functioned as the primary mode of service delivery before the advent
of government intervention, and where anarchy, violence, military, and religious solutions are not deemed to be acceptable. During this time, separate narratives of market failure and government failure, as discussed above, were developed to explain why
neither markets nor governments functioned exactly as their ideal
forms would suggest.

The principal difference between analyses of market failure and
government failure is that market failure presumes that markets
will function efficiently and as intended under most circumstances, but that situations can arise that can cause markets to fail.
Government failure, on the other hand, presumes the opposite –
that governments will inevitably fail at all tasks and endeavours.
Both Wolf's (1987; 1988) and Le Grand's (1991) theories of government failure argue that all government activity will lead to failure, and differences between the theories are related to why this is
and which market mechanisms can best be used to replace government intervention.

In reality, markets and governments are both essential components of a liberal democratic state and of a developed economy. In
some countries, notably Switzerland (Trampusch and Mach 2011),
South Korea (Lee 1992), and Singapore (Haque 2004), institution-

alized collaboration of governments and private firms has historically produced sustained economic growth and dramatic improve-
ments in living standards. More importantly, the dichotomy
between market mechanisms and government intervention is no
longer as distinct as it may have been in the past. In the current era
of governance, the debate has transitioned from "whether old-style
public intervention is better than the free market, or vice versa" to
"the ways in which state and market can be integrated" (Goodwin
1998, 5). Newer conceptions of governance are supposed to bridge
the ideological gap between governments and markets, to allow
them to collaborate rather than to antagonize each other (Jessop
2000, 16–18) or to operate in parallel.

In light of this, separate accounts of market and government
failure are no longer sufficient to represent the dynamics of interaction between governments, corporations, and society. However,
the concept of *governance* failure has yet to be fully articulated.
Early examples include Dixon and Dogan (2002, 175), who define
governance failure as the "perceived ineffectiveness of governance
processes," but their use of the word "governance" is in the traditional, more simple sense of governing (as opposed to the notion
of cooperative, delegated, multilateral, and decentralized governing that I have associated with the word "governance" so far in this
book); thus, they are referring to all forms of governing including
government and market, as well as mixed forms of governance.
Dixon and Dogan's treatment of the subject involves a philo-
sophical approach to the epistemological and ontological issues of
the interaction between the governed and their governors, and
although they offer a thorough discussion of the effects of all
modes of governance failure on this interaction, they do not
explore the conditions for or the causes of failure.

Without offering an actual set of criteria for failure, Jessop (1998;
2000) describes what a more complete description of governance
failure might look like: since governance combines the economic
goals of the market with the social goals of the state, governance
failure would likely emerge as a failure in both economic and
social/political terms. Jessop (2000, 17) further argues that, since
the point of governance is to provide flexibility to decision-making
structures (as opposed to the rigid structures of the state bureau-

cracy or the strict microeconomic laws of the market), a general theory of governance failure might prove to be elusive. However, Jessop's conclusions take the defeatist position that all attempts at governance will inevitably fail, since the objectives of the state and the objectives of private sector corporations will never be completely aligned. This position, like that of government failure theorists, is not conducive to theory-building, because if governance is liable to fail under all circumstances, constructing a theory of when and how governance can fail is unnecessary – it will simply always fail. This point of view, taken to its logical extreme, also raises curious questions such as whether or not the best course of action would be to do away with governance entirely and find some other mode of state-society interaction to replace it.

Bovens, 't Hart, and Peters (2001) present an ambitious attempt to analyze governance failure, as well as governance success, using a comparative approach in Western Europe. However, what these authors refer to as "governance failure" might more aptly be called "policy failure," as it pertains directly to the "effectiveness, efficiency and resilience of the specific policies being evaluated" and their political interpretations (Bovens et al. 2001, 20). While their study is situated in the context of the shift to a cooperative mode of governance in which the public and private sectors are increasingly collaborating in the delivery of public services and in the regulation of national economies, the authors' focus is on how national governments tackle specific social and economic problems – and not on the factors that contribute to failure in governance partnerships.

The concept of governance failure is advanced further by Arnouts and Arts's (2009) study on bird species and habitat conservation policy in the Netherlands. Arnouts and Arts offer a preliminary theory of governance failure, in which governance structures can expect to succumb to four kinds of failure: "actor overload," in which the presence of too many actors involved in a policy area can cause a breakdown in the function of a governance network; "power struggles," in which conflict occurs over which actors are responsible for which decisions; "conflicting discourses," where different actors may interpret the goals of the policy process differently; and "unclear rules," where confusion over the rules of interaction between the actors occurs. However, this account is handicapped by two shortcomings. First, these four metrics are somewhat arbitrarily defined and unmeasurable. How many actors are necessary to cause an overload? How unclear do rules need to be in order for a failure to occur? Unfortunately, governance failure itself is never satisfactorily defined, so these questions are impossible to answer. Secondly, the authors' assumption from the beginning is that failure is an inevitable outcome of governance – this is their initial hypothesis and is also reflected in their conclusions.

Governance, in the sense that I am using the word here, can be defined as a combination of markets and governments working together through some blend of structured and unstructured interaction. Therefore, if governance can fail anywhere it must be by failing to allow market-government collaboration to happen. Of course, governance does not necessarily imply deliberate, hierarchical consensus-building (although it can); in many cases, government and non-government actors reach compromises through negotiation, bargaining, preference-pooling, log-rolling, and competition. When governance functions smoothly, this bargaining and competition gravitates toward a dynamic equilibrium that can produce policy outputs. A governance failure can be said to occur when this equilibrium is disrupted, that is, when a governance regime results in unstable antagonism between corresponding public and private sector actors. Governance has failed completely when cooperation for mutual benefit – organized or otherwise – ceases to happen.

Governance arrangements can last for long periods of time and can produce continuous policy outputs. For example, over the past twenty years, international airports in Canada (all of which had previously been controlled directly by the federal government) have been turned over to independent, privately managed, not-for-profit airport authorities. This system has produced functioning airports that continue to cooperate with the federal government on issues such as the long-term leasing of land and property, infrastructure expansion, and environmental protection (Gillen and Morrison 2004; Oum et al. 2006; Padova 2007). In other words, in the case of airport restructuring in Canada, governance has achieved its policy objectives through an interactive collaboration of market actors and government, and therefore cannot be considered a governance failure. A normative evaluation of the successes of this governance regime – for example, whether semi-privatized airports are better or worse than airports that are run directly by governments – would have to be assessed in terms of who benefits from the regime, and how, and how much.

Of course, not all governance arrangements are harmonious and governance failure does happen. Borins (1986) recounts the stories of several governance failures in mixed enterprise in Canada, in which the government subsidized or invested in private corporations. In all of Borins's cases, the partnership ended either in bankruptcy or in the sale of the government's interest in the company. In the United States, a P3 arrangement for express toll lanes on California State Route 91 led to legal action between the public sector and private sector partners, and resulted in the purchase of the entire asset by the California Department of Transportation (Garvin and Bosso 2008). Also in the US, the multi-decade collaboration between the government and the private sector to develop alternative energy sources, including liquefied coal and fusion reactors, ended without ever producing a useful product (Grossman 2009). Arguably, the 2008–09 economic crisis and associated failures of the banking sectors in many countries could be considered a governance failure, as relaxed banking regulations resulted in an unsustainable governance regime (Aikins 2009). In all of these cases, market-government collaboration to achieve policy goals was not attained, and distributional outcomes produced negative results for users in particular and citizens in general (in the form of a loss of money to the public purse).

Governance failure can be a terminal position. For instance, in the case of the Bricklin sports car that was produced through a joint venture between the provincial government of New Brunswick and the private sector, governance failure was in fact an end point as it resulted in the termination of the project (Borins 1986). In some cases, governance failure can have repercussions that are felt beyond the lifespan of the initial partnership, as in the "fast ferry fiasco" in which the province of British Columbia lost about $500 million producing three aluminum ferries that were permanently taken out of service shortly after

delivery (Greve 2011, 955). In this example, a firm public perception of government waste will likely have an impact on future
transportation policy in British Columbia for many years into
the future.

However, governance failure is not necessarily terminal in every
case. It is possible that governance failures might be resolved; this
may have happened, for example, in the case of the rail link to
Brisbane's airport (Lilley and de Giorgio 2004, 39), which experienced disastrously low ridership but has since recovered, due in
part to a renegotiated P3 contract. In other examples, such as
Canada Post's entry into the courier industry through its acquisition of Purolator, some minor disputes arose between the public
and private sectors that would qualify as conflict, but this did not
lead to major consequences for the policy network that could be
identified as "failure" (see Toulin 1999; Nafziger and Wanak 2009
for example).

In other words, like failures of government, market, or policy,
governance failures can vary in degree, in magnitude of consequences, and in potential for recovery. Some governance failures
will have repercussions that have lasting effects, while others can
be resolved with only minor consequences. However, the same
definition of failure applies to all cases, and even those with the
potential for resolution can still be considered failures during the
time that the governance arrangement fails to achieve its objectives. From an academic perspective, however, students of governance would probably concern themselves most with governance
failures that have permanent and nontrivial consequences.

GOVERNANCE THROUGH POLICY NETWORKS

Many informal governance systems involve the use of non-state
actors operating in horizontal, dynamic regimes called "policy networks" that function under a convention of implied rules rather
than binding contract obligations (Van Waarden 1992; Thatcher
1998; Sørensen and Torfing 2007a; Koppenjan et al. 2009). Policy
networks are composed of some state actors and institutions but
also include non-state organizations, and some authors describe a
spectrum of formality-informality and hierarchy-horizontality,
with different networks operating at different points along each

continuum (Coleman and Perl 1999; Rhodes 2006). Nearly all authors agree that the basis for cohesion in policy networks is resource interdependence between network participants (Klijn and Koppenjan 2000; Adam and Kriesi 2007; Hertting 2007; Compston 2009).

Policy networks are of particular importance to a discussion of the role of the state in the governance of state-society relations. While welfare state critics like Savas (2000) take a materialist perspective in arguing that the privatization of welfare activities is a superior and logical next step in the ongoing re-examination of a government's role in directing society, policy network scholars describe an alternative mode of governance in which private sector actors and government agencies collaborate on public policy development and delivery. Instead of a complete retrenchment of the government from social policy formulation and implementation, policy networks offer evidence that it is possible for government entities and non-state actors to cooperate on the conceptual inputs that go into policy-making as well as the technical outputs that are involved in policy implementation. Policy networks exist in many countries in a variety of industries, such as telecom, energy, criminal justice, minerals extraction, and transportation.

A defining quality of policy networks is that they are horizontal interactions of (not necessarily equal) participants – unlike the strict vertical hierarchy of bureaucracy (Van Waarden 1992; Thatcher 1998, 398; Koppenjan et al. 2009). However, because of the absence of established hierarchy, policy networks are vulnerable to manipulation by governments, especially when a state is required to assert its sovereignty in a policy area (Atkinson and Coleman 1992; Pierre and Peters 2000; Koppenjan et al. 2009). For example, the market for new homes in Australia is a regulated, but largely autonomous, industry; nevertheless, when the federal government decides to make a change to the rules of operation, as it did when it raised interest rates on foreign owners of residential property in 2015, repercussions are felt throughout the industry (Hutchens and Macken 2015).

More generally, many authors steadfastly argue that even in a governance mode of policy-making, the state retains the sovereign power to step in and change or enforce policies against the settlements reached by policy networks (Atkinson and Coleman 1992; Pierre and Peters 2000; Koppenjan et al. 2009). A potent example of this occurred in Canada in 2010, when the federal government decided to overrule the Canadian Radio-television Telecommunications Commission on the entry of Wind Mobile to the Canadian wireless telecom market (see Mayeda 2010 for a more detailed report of the incident).

As policy networks are informal governance arrangements, it stands to reason that they could potentially result in governance failure. Even though many policy networks are unorganized and can rely on non-collaborative elements such as competition (Sørensen and Torfing 2005, 203), the active participation of network members is fundamental to the network's operation. When network actors refuse to participate, a policy network will degenerate into a governance failure, and then either the network will be abandoned or the government will be required to exercise some form of "metagovernance" (Sørensen and Torfing 2007b, 110) to rescue the network by imposing some structure. Governments can encourage network participation by formalizing the rules of interaction, by offering incentives to participate, or by force through regulatory or legislative control.

Koppenjan (2007, 150–1) has theorized that network function depends on a balance between conflict and consensus, both of which are critical elements of network interaction. If there is insufficient conflict, a network will stagnate and become essentially useless, because agonistic interaction, such as competition and bargaining, is crucial for innovation. However, too much conflict will cause the network to disintegrate, because it will prevent interaction entirely or because it will effectively cause network actors to avoid participating. Networks will either reach an equilibrium where they have a balance of conflict and consensus that allows interaction to become sustainable (with the presumption that there are many points along a spectrum in which this can occur, owing to the idiosyncrasies of a particular network's composition and context) or they will gravitate toward one extreme or the other and result in governance failure.

These outcomes of failure as proposed by Koppenjan have different implications for governance: a stagnant or dysfunctional policy network can still produce outputs, but these outputs may not align with a government's (or society's) priorities in that sector, and without intervention this can result in a long term static position. This is what happened in the automotive industry in the US in the 1990s, when governance arrangements were attempted for the development of high efficiency automobiles (Sperling 2001; Perl and Dunn 2007; Grossman 2009). In that example, hundreds of millions of dollars were spent on a public-private governance regime to develop American-made cars with very high fuel efficiency, but the outputs of the network resulted instead in a proliferation of larger and less fuel efficient sports utility vehicles from American companies and a limited number of fuel efficient models from Japanese manufacturers. On the other hand, a network that has experienced total collapse will by definition cease to produce policy outputs at all.

The extension of this discussion to P3s is somewhat problematic, because at first glance it is unclear whether or not public-private partnerships are a form of policy network. Initial scholarship on the issue seems to suggest that they are (see Teisman and Klijn 2002 for example): a P3 can be viewed as a network consisting of a private sector partner (often actually a consortium of private interests) and some combination of various levels of government and related agencies, collaborating to achieve one or more policy objectives. This multitude of actors on both the public and private sector sides lends itself readily to a model of network governance. On the other hand, the contractual nature of the partnership arrangement negates the supposed advantages of a policy network: dynamic flexibility and the absence of hierarchy (Hodge and Bowman 2004, 205). The binding partnership contract that is an inherent component of P3s will necessarily have an influence on the interaction of P3 partners, which may alter the function of the partnership so as to distinguish it fundamentally from policy networks.

However, while policy networks are informal collaborative arrangements between the public and private sectors, they are complex systems that could include some formalized relationships as well. For example, a private corporation might have a contract with a particular US state for the operation of a single prison within that state, but it might then also be part of a greater network of firms, governments, regulatory agencies, and trade organizations that is collectively responsible for nation-wide prison policy in what some have termed the "prison-industrial complex" (Schlosser 1998). Therefore, it may be possible to conceive of nested policy networks, in which smaller, tighter units of interaction exist within concentric or perhaps overlapping policy subsystems. Seen from this perspective, P3s may exist as very specific governance arrangements nested within much larger networks whose boundaries may be less precise. While the activity of the actors within the P3 may be delineated by an official contract, their interaction can still contribute to the formulation and implementation of policy within the greater subsystem.

Both the Canada Line and the Sydney Airport Link can be viewed in these terms. In Vancouver, the actors within the official Canada Line partnership have specific duties and responsibilities, but their interactions form only a small component of a greater policy network that governs urban transit in the Metro Vancouver region (which in turn contributes to transportation policy in British Columbia, which in turn forms part of a greater policy subsystem that has an impact on urban development and environmental policy in British Columbia and Canada). The position of the Canada Line as a nested policy network within a greater system of networks is illustrated in Figure 3.1. In Sydney, the Airport Link P3 was influenced by multiple actors who were situated within a greater governance network, but this network failed to function to its fullest potential.

In summary, governance failure can occur in both formalized governance arrangements or in informal networks. In formal arrangements, governance failure can result in ongoing conflict between partners bound by a contractual agreement. In informal networks, often called policy networks, failure results in either long term stagnation or in the termination of the network, unless a public sector authority intervenes to stabilize the network and restore collaboration. Governance failure may have pecuniary consequences, social/political consequences, or both, but regardless of the types of consequences that failure may generate, governance arrangements are considered to have failed when the interaction between the public and private sectors is no longer sustainable –

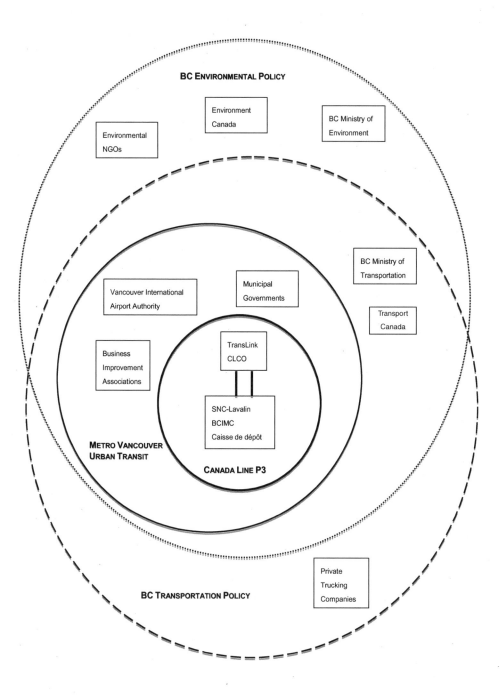

Figure 3.1 Nested policy networks in British Columbia

in other words, when it is no longer stable over time and cannot remain faithful to its original objectives without major intervention from external forces (Patashnik 2003, 207).

THE ROLE OF THE STATE

Although there are notable exceptions (see Knill and Lehmkuhl 2002 for example), many scholars maintain that despite the shift from government to governance that has occurred over the last thirty years, national governments remain not only relevant, but also retain their position as the dominant authority within the national sphere (Atkinson and Coleman 1992, 167–8; Pierre and Peters 2000). This perspective has some appeal: how did many Western democracies make the transition from government to governance, if not through deliberate policy choices enforced by law, such as widespread industrial deregulation and the sale of state-owned assets? Governments may have delegated decision making for some areas of public policy to private entities, but they have never relinquished their legislative capacity or their Weberian monopoly on the legitimate use of violence. Even in residual areas of policy, where governments may not have created or enforced any official rules as of yet, they reserve the ability to intervene should the need arise. This is illustrated by the example of the internet, which is largely unregulated in Western states but which could be regulated much more forcefully should governments ever decide to – as evidenced by the crackdown on media piracy that has accelerated in some countries in recent years.

In other words, governments are not merely passive bystanders to the effects of governance and to the implications of governance failure. They are active participants in both the development of governance arrangements for public services and for their implementation and ongoing delivery to society. Logically, then, if we are interested in the consequences of governance failure then we are also interested in the state's active role in contributing to or in preventing it. Questions about failures in governance should therefore look to the responsibility of the partners in ensuring that governance arrangements succeed, and the government, which bears a natural responsibility to its polity, carries a heavier burden in actively endeavouring to prevent governance failure. Therefore, the question "If governance failure does happen, how can it be prevented or avoided?" can be more usefully reformulated as "If governance failure does happen, how can the government act to prevent or avoid it?"

Of course, once precedents have been set, and once binding agreements have been signed, the political costs of government intervention in governance arrangements can be significant, especially when intervention strategies are perceived as reducing economic growth, restricting civil liberties, or increasing public expenditures. In some cases, the state's ability to interfere with a governance system may be restricted to emergency situations, such as in response to terrorist attacks or following a global financial crisis. Although governments terminate contracts with private corporations on a regular basis, doing so within the legal bounds of the contract usually entails significant financial penalties. For example, the city of Ottawa was forced to pay around $40 million to a consortium of transportation companies after it cancelled a light rail expansion project in 2006 (Greenberg 2011). In Australia, Sydney's city council paid $5 million in an out-of-court settlement after it was sued by a company whose contract to install street lighting throughout the city was cancelled (McClymont 2007). In a more extreme example, when the Canadian federal government terminated its contract with European Helicopter Industries to replace its aging fleet of Sea King military helicopters, it paid penalties of almost $500 million (Plamondon 2010, xv).

There are two ways to look at this. On the one hand, the government has never abdicated its role as the ultimate authority in national affairs. In the words of Pierre and Peters (2000, 25), "the state, despite persistent rumours to the contrary, remains the key political actor in society and the predominant expression of collective interests." On the other hand, states in an era of governance will be bound by cultural and political forces that will constrain their actions in many circumstances (Mayntz 1993). Governments will be forced to consider significant intervention in some governance regimes to be a strategy of last resort.

The situation is different on the smaller scale. In the vast majority of governance arrangements, including informal arrangements like policy networks and contract-bound relationships like P3s, governments retain the capacity to exert at least some control. This is because minor interventions, such as directing contract negotiations or subtle changes to regulation, can be implemented in small, occasional increments that may avoid attention but that can produce consequential results. Although it is true that major intervention could create controversy in some instances, regular small-scale action is a fundamental part of the state's role in governance. This is evidenced by the federal government's periodic intervention in the Canadian mortgage market over the last ten years, which despite some minor disapproval voiced mainly by the construction industry (see Marr 2012 for example) has been accepted by the private banks without major resistance. Similar examples of incremental rule changes abound in many countries and in many industries, including financial regulation in the EU (Quaglia 2012, 521), nutritional information labelling in the US (Kiesel et al. 2011), and tobacco advertising in Australia (Mitchell and Studdert 2012, 262), just to name a few.

Markets and governments may be independent systems that can in some cases operate autonomously, but governance arrangements by definition require the active cooperation of both market actors and governments at the same time. They are not self-sufficient or self-sustaining systems. In addition, markets are, also by definition, not centrally controlled, and market actors in a governance regime will not necessarily act as a unified bloc. While each actor in a governance system may derive benefits from the arrangement, a central goal or collective motive for collaboration will not develop spontaneously, not for the system as a whole and especially not among the private sector actors alone. Moreover, as has been noted previously, in many cases the public and private sector actors may have different objectives that are not completely in alignment.

Putting these last few points together we find that:

1 Governments have ultimate authority for statecraft, including the ability to intervene in established governance regimes.

2 Although radical intervention by governments in governance systems may be politically difficult, incremental action is not only possible but is a form of intervention that is widely used by many governments in numerous policy areas.

3 Due to the participation of market-based actors, governance regimes have no inherent leadership.

4 Because of the different needs and goals of the public and private sectors, governance regimes may have no central objectives that all participants can agree on.

In short, governments have a direct role to play in governance, and not only as willing participants in a collaborative effort. They must also act as executive authorities with immediate responsibility for the collaboration's smooth operation, in order to direct activity and to determine the rules of participation, even if mostly in small but periodic increments. In addition, governments must function as distant sovereigns with ultimate emergency powers, ready to intervene with radical directives when the situation calls for it. These roles apply to governments themselves as well as to public sector agencies to whom they may delegate immediate responsibility for particular areas of public policy or for the implementation of specific projects.

If government responsibility is key to the proper function of governance systems, then it stands to reason that an effective way to achieve governance failure is by constraining or eliminating the state's role in directing a particular governance arrangement. Governance systems require sufficient leadership from the state, without which they will fail. This can happen through neglect or through error, but when governance failure occurs, it is because the government partners did not supply the amount of leadership required for that particular governance arrangement.

But how much is "sufficient" leadership? Unfortunately, policy leadership is not something that exists in discrete units. It does not lend itself easily to quantitative measurement; therefore, identifying the critical point at which leadership becomes sufficient to avoid a governance failure is likely not possible. The level of intervention that is required by the public sector partners in a governance arrangement will depend on the magni-

tude of the weaknesses presented by the structure of the arrangement. A public-private partnership for infrastructure involving a
long-term contract, high levels of capital investment, revenue
guarantees for the private sector, or other elements that are governance pressure points might require hands-on leadership of
day-to-day activities and substantial planning and research; in
other sectors, such as telecom, in which market principles are
more influential because of the direct relationship between producers and consumers, a governance arrangement may function
with only some legislated rules and a public sector oversight
body. Policy leadership will be crucial in either case, but the
level of involvement of the public sector will depend on the
demands of the arrangement.

CONCLUSION

By obstructing public policy outputs, governance failure can lead
to significant financial loss, opportunity cost, and depletion of
resources. Furthermore, it can create distrust between public and
private sector actors that may lead to an unwillingness to collaborate in the future. This would significantly limit the state's ability
to provide public services in an era where a reliance on governance
strategies has become the norm. More directly, a failure in a particular governance arrangement means that the objectives of that
arrangement are not being met, which implies that some objective
of public policy has not been achieved. On a macroscopic level,
governance failure can directly erode the powers of democracy by
undermining the ability of elected representatives to enact and
enforce legislation. Governance failures can also represent financial loss for private sector partners, which may have an impact on
the general economy.

There are various ways that governments can employ policy
leadership and avoid failure in governance arrangements. In the
chapters that follow, I will examine two very similar cases of public-private partnerships in transportation, one of which experienced governance failure due to a lack of policy leadership from
the public sector. In the other case, three different policy leadership strategies – employed simultaneously – prevented governance
failure from happening.

4

Case Studies

P3s have been in use in the transportation sector for many years, and continue to be a popular method of service and infrastructure delivery in many jurisdictions. In Canada, road and bridge infrastructure is the preferred mode, and examples abound: the Confederation Bridge link between Prince Edward Island and New Brunswick (Garvin and Bosso 2008, 162), Vancouver's "Sea-to-Sky" highway from Vancouver to Whistler (Cohn 2008), the Golden Ears bridge linking Maple Ridge and Langley, British Columbia (Greater Vancouver Transportation Authority 2006), Edmonton's Anthony Henday Drive Ring Road (Alberta Transportation 2012), and Ontario's Highway 407 (Mylvaganam and Borins 2004), to name a few. Australia has a history of using P3s for transit, including Brisbane's Airtrain, Sydney's light rail system, and passenger rail in Melbourne (Williams et al. 2005), as well as for roadways: the Cross City Tunnel in Sydney (Siemiatycki 2010), the CityLink system in Melbourne (Hodge and Bowman 2004), and the Clem Jones and Airport Link tunnels in Brisbane (Mols 2010) were all P3 projects.

The two cases compared here are the Canada Line in Vancouver, Canada and the Sydney Airport Link in Sydney, Australia. Both of these are major pieces of urban transportation infrastructure. Both were implemented through public-private partnerships in which private sector consortia invested substantial amounts of capital in exchange for sole responsibility for construction and thirty-year operating concessions. However, as has been mentioned in previous chapters, the case of the Canada Line was largely a success while the Sydney Airport Link experienced governance failure. The purpose of this chapter is to describe the history, context, organizational layout, and relevant technical details of the two cases in order to provide some background for the chapters that follow.

THE CANADA LINE

The Canada Line, previously known as the Richmond-Airport-Vancouver Line or RAV Line, is a 19 km rail rapid transit line that connects downtown Vancouver to the Vancouver International Airport and to Richmond, British Columbia, a nearby suburb. It has 16 stations, all of which opened for operation on the same day on 17 August 2009. At about $2.5 billion, the Canada Line was, at the time, the biggest infrastructure project ever undertaken in the province of British Columbia (British Columbia 2009).

The Canada Line is fully integrated into Greater Vancouver's public transit network. In addition to major connectivity with surrounding bus routes (many of which feed directly to the line), the Canada Line functions as an extension of Vancouver's SkyTrain urban rail network: passengers can use the same ticket products on the Canada Line that they would purchase for the SkyTrain, and Canada Line stations are placed in locations that facilitate connection to the other lines when possible. However, the Canada Line does not use the same technology as the rest of SkyTrain, and the vehicles are not interchangeable. Consequently, for operating purposes the Canada Line is a stand-alone branch of a greater urban transit system.

Studies into the possibility and desirability of a rapid transit connection between Vancouver and Richmond date back as far as 1970, but it was only after the creation of TransLink in 1999 that real efforts began to take shape (RAV Project Management Ltd. 2003, 20).[1] The creation of TransLink was a significant turn of

---

1 When it was created in 1999, the official name was the Greater Vancouver Transportation Authority. Since a restructuring in 2007, its legal name is now the South Coast British Columbia Transportation Authority. However, the organization has always operated under the name TransLink, so to avoid confusion, that is the name I will use here.

events in regional transportation policy in Vancouver, because prior to 1999, public transit for the entire province of British Columbia was run by B.C. Transit, a provincial Crown corporation headquartered in the provincial capital of Victoria (Harcourt and Cameron 2007). With the advent of TransLink, executive decision making for public transit was relocated from the provincial level to the local level, as TransLink was to be governed by a board of directors composed of mayors and city councillors from Greater Vancouver's twenty-one separate municipalities.[2] One of the major priorities that emerged from the regionally directed organization's first Strategic Transportation Plan in 2000 was the creation of a Richmond to Vancouver rapid transit link (RAV Project Management Ltd. 2003, 21).

The Canada Line was the result of the collaboration of a number of independent organizations from the public and private sectors. Many actors, including governments, public sector agencies, and private corporations had a vested interest in the outcome of this project. Many of these relationships were formalized through written agreements, creating an intricate web of roles and responsibilities for the participating organizations. An organizational chart of the various participants is given in Figure 4.1.[3]

On the private sector side, several private corporations placed bids for the right to design, build, finance, and operate the Canada Line. There was a multi-stage, multi-year public tender process in which the number of competing candidates from the private sector was progressively reduced at each stage. The winning proponent – a consortium consisting of the Quebec-based engineering firm SNC-Lavalin, the British Columbia Investment Management Corporation (British Columbia's public sector employee pension fund), and the Caisse de dépôt et placement du Québec (Quebec's public sector employee pension fund) – signed a contract to build the Canada Line and operate the service until the

2 This governance format lasted until TransLink was restructured in 2007, an incident that will be described in more detail later.

3 All diagrams, including maps, are of my own creation based on information uncovered through my research, and are for illustrative purposes only. They are in no way official diagrams and have not been endorsed by the organizations they refer to.

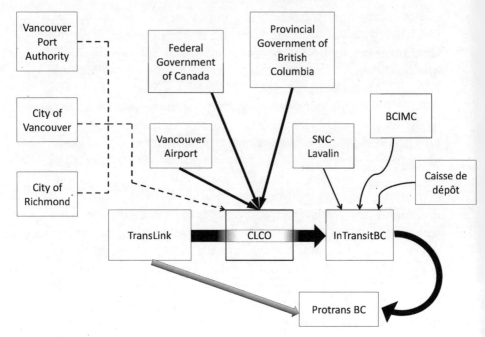

Figure 4.1 Organizational chart of the Canada Line

year 2040. The private sector partners, acting through a special purpose corporation called InTransit BC, in which each partner has a one-third share, invested $138 million in equity and $688 million in loans from international banks (Canada Line Rapid Transit Inc. 2006, 12). InTransit then contracted SNC-Lavalin to lead the construction phase, and later created a separate subsidiary named Protrans BC to manage the subsequent operation of the line.

Although final authority for the Canada Line falls to the provincial government, the public sector "partner" is actually a group of participants as well. The provincial government, the federal government, the city of Vancouver, the Vancouver Airport Authority, and TransLink all contributed funding to the project. Additional stakeholders, such as the Vancouver Port Authority and the City of Richmond, were included for consultation purposes at many crucial decision-making junctures. Canada Line Rapid Transit Inc. (sometimes known as CLRT, but more commonly CLCO, an abbreviation of "Canada Line Company"), was created by the provincial government to provide project management services. CLCO was officially owned entirely by TransLink, but it operated with considerable independence. Once the Canada Line went into operation, CLCO was dissolved.

As is to be expected, relationships between the public sector participants in the Canada Line project were complicated. CLCO was wholly owned by TransLink, which has always been a statutory creation of the provincial government. The provincial government has exclusive powers over regional transportation, but the federal government can (and did, in this case) exert some influence by offering or denying funding contributions. The cities of Vancouver, Richmond, and the metropolitan governments are all constitutionally under the jurisdiction of the provincial government. The Vancouver Port Authority is an agency of the federal government under the jurisdiction of the federal ministry of transportation. The Vancouver Airport Authority is a private not-for-profit corporation mandated by the federal government to oversee airport operations. In day-to-day activity, these entities all operate independently; however, jurisdictional hierarchy allows for intervention from superior organizations from time to time. In order to avoid destructive conflict among the various public sector participants, CLCO was tasked with brokering their cooperation and handling all interaction with the private sector partners (this function of CLCO will be the subject of chapter 7). Relationships between the Canada Line's public sector organizations are shown in Figure 4.2.

The construction phase of the Canada Line project was structured as a fixed-price design-build contract, which means that the private contractor was responsible for engineering and construction and all costs associated with those activities except for some costs that were specifically allocated to the public sector partner. The public sector funding partners, through CLCO, made periodic milestone payments to InTransit throughout the construction period. In this way, construction risk was intended to be divided such that the bulk of the risk was carried by the private sector partner (Canada Line Rapid Transit Inc. 2006, 12).

For the thirty-one-year operating phase, Protrans BC is responsible for the operation of the line, but they must work in close contact with TransLink, as the Canada Line is an integrated component of the regional transportation network. Payments are made

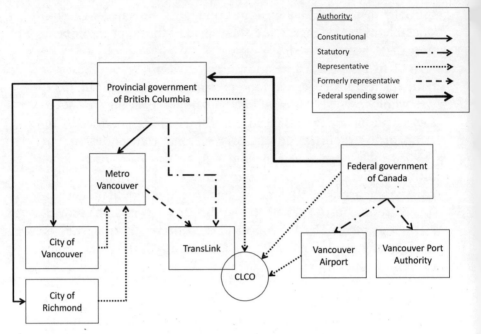

Figure 4.2 Relationships between the Canada Line's public sector organizations

regularly from TransLink to Protrans BC, 70 per cent of which is calculated based on the "availability" of service, 20 per cent on "quality," and 10 per cent on "achievement of ridership forecasts" (Canada Line 2006). However, specific details and the formulae used for calculation are not publicly available, as they are considered to be commercially sensitive information and have been redacted from public copies of the Canada Line concession agreement (see RAV Project Management Ltd. 2005a: Schedule 11, for example). TransLink retains ownership of the fixed assets, including the tunnels and most of the stations, while InTransit owns the rolling stock (Canada Line Rapid Transit Inc. 2006, 6). The Vancouver International Airport owns the fixed infrastructure on Sea Island (where the airport is located) in addition to Bridgeport Station in the city of Richmond, but leases both to TransLink for a nominal amount (Canada Line 2006). Again, complete details of the financial arrangement are confidential and are kept hidden from public view.

Partnerships BC, a provincially owned corporation whose mandate is to "encourage the development of the public-private partnership market in British Columbia" and to "structure and implement public-private partnership solutions which serve the public interest" (British Columbia 2007), functioned as advisor to both the public and private sector partners. Partnerships BC aided in the preparation of the public sector comparator, a financial analysis tool that is commonly used for "value for money" analysis of P3 projects (Siemiatycki 2010, 48). Although most of my interview respondents suggested or directly commented that the role of Partnerships BC in the Canada Line process was minimal at best, this still represents an added complexity to the diverse nature of the partnership arrangement for Canada Line.

The Canada Line has enjoyed popularity with the general public since it was announced as a transportation priority. Surveys continuously showed it was a popular choice for public investment in transportation infrastructure, in Vancouver and Richmond, as well as in other suburbs of the Greater Vancouver area (Kirk and Co. 2003; Synovate 2003, 2004; Braid 2004). Contrary to evidence that transportation megaprojects frequently fail to attain their forecasted ridership levels (Flyvbjerg et al. 2003), the Canada Line was successful from the beginning: in 2010, after one year of service, its daily weekday average was 104,000 passengers per day – well beyond its predicted level for 2010 and more than 4 per cent above its expected average for 2013 (Sinoski 2010). In other words, the public's initial enthusiasm for the Canada Line continued into its operating period, and the expert consultants who prepared ridership estimates and polling data were proven to be correct regarding how high the demand for the line would be. In addition, the line opened for service several months early, and numerous reports of its being "on budget" (e.g., British Columbia 2010) have never been forcefully disputed.

This popularity comes in spite of considerable controversy over the design and procurement of the system that nearly caused the project to be cancelled in its early stages. Friction between the provincial government and the assembly of mayors of the metropolitan region of Vancouver – then called the Greater Vancouver Regional District, but now (and hereafter in this text) referred to as Metro Vancouver – appears to be an inherent element in provincial-municipal relations in British Columbia, even before the creation of TransLink or the inception of the Canada Line, and irrespective of the political parties in power (Harcourt and Cameron 2007). This inter-governmental friction reappeared during the early stages of the development of the Canada Line, when disagreements over the funding structure of the project were made public. After the province announced that provincial funding for the Canada Line would be contingent on the project's structure as a P3, both Vancouver's city council (Bula 2003a) and Metro Vancouver (Bula 2003b) voted in favour of the project but publicly opposed the P3 requirement, while the board of directors of TransLink voted in favour of the P3 format. Several further dramatic votes at the regional level followed, in which the board of TransLink twice voted not to continue the project and then later revived the debate so as to be able to vote on it a third time. The project was narrowly approved, and in the end, the requirement of a P3 architecture for the project was formalized in the provincial funding agreement (British Columbia 2005).

In addition to the debate over the use of a P3 arrangement, the conflict between the levels of government contained further political motivations. According to Larry Campbell, then mayor of Vancouver, although local politicians who favoured the political left were opposed to the use of P3, those on the right were dissatisfied with the proposal's expanding costs, and there was generally a sentiment among the region's mayors that the Richmond-to-Vancouver line was being prioritized ahead of rapid transit projects to other municipalities that had been considered more important in the region's strategic transportation plan (quoted in Bula 2004a). However, the increased publicity for the Canada Line that was produced by this antagonism between the provincial and municipal or regional levels of government arguably allowed for increased public awareness of the project, as the debate was covered extensively by the local media (e.g., Boei 2004).

A further public debate on the project concerned the route and alignment. The provincial government, the project management team, and the TransLink executive all advocated a grade-separated rail line down Cambie Street in Vancouver, which is a central traffic corridor with a wide boulevard and with several major destinations, such as shopping districts and hospitals (RAV Project Management Ltd. 2003). Many critics favoured a less expensive at-grade light rail system that would have followed an abandoned freight right-of-way along the more residential Arbutus Street (Krangle 2003). Ironically, serious consideration of the light rail option is what led the local governments to return to the provincial government's original recommendation (including the P3 requirement for provincial funding), since consultant reports on ridership for the light rail alignment were considerably lower than those that had been reported for a dedicated right-of-way along Cambie Street (Bula 2004b). While the Canada Line has variously been referred to as "light rail" (e.g., Demetri 2007), it is not light rail in the sense that this term is usually used in transportation planning circles, where it denotes at-grade systems in which tracks are embedded in paved motorways and trains sometimes or always share the right-of-way with automobile traffic (Ruffilli 2010, 2). The Canada Line is grade-separated along its entire length, either in tunnel or on elevated guideways (except for a short stretch at Vancouver International Airport, where the Canada Line runs at-grade alongside Grant McConachie Way. However, the Canada Line does not intersect or interfere with automobile traffic at any point along this segment of the line). A comparison of the proposed routes is shown in Figure 4.3, and a map of the Canada Line as it was eventually built is given in Figure 4.4.

And lastly, the decision to use a grade-separated alignment along Cambie Street produced its own controversy. CLCO and TransLink had frequently stated that any tunnel through residential districts in Vancouver would likely be bored, in which machinery is lowered into the ground, a tunnel is excavated under the street, and the operation emerges at the other end without much disturbance to street-level activity except at the locations of the stations. However, as the P3 for the Canada Line incorporated a design-build component, the private sector proponents had the freedom to propose their own technology and construction methods if that would lower their costs without deviating from the project's essential elements. In fact, the winning private sector bid proposed to use the "cut and cover" method for tunnelling in residential Vancouver, in which a deep trench is exposed in the middle of the street, the tunnel's concrete structure is poured from the top, and then the road is closed and paved once the tunnel (or a section of

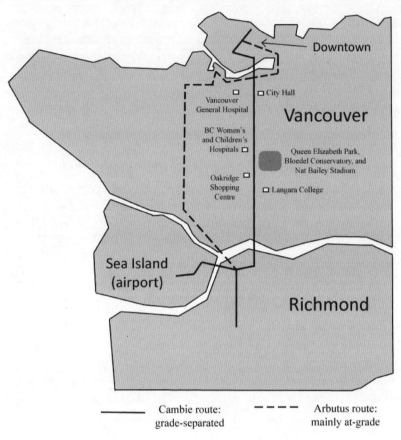

Figure 4.3 Proposed route of Vancouver's Canada Line

the tunnel) is completed. Cut and cover is far less expensive than tunnel boring, but it is dramatically more intrusive to the daily lives of people and businesses in the area.

Neither CLCO nor TransLink made any initial public announcements that the final chosen method of construction was different than what had been suggested earlier. Instead, an image of the tunnel alignment was released to the public in January 2005 that showed a stacked tunnel arrangement, which would not have been possible to construct through tunnel boring, and this prompted public declarations by local residents and political opponents that they had been deceived (Boei 2005). Angry business owners along

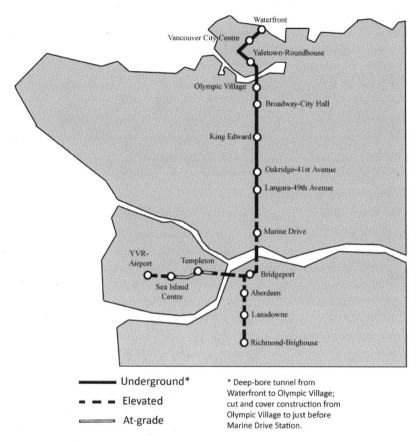

Figure 4.4 Vancouver's Canada Line as it was eventually built

Cambie Street took the matter to court in an attempt to halt construction of the line, but they were ultimately unsuccessful, as their
appeals went as far as the Supreme Court of Canada but were dismissed at that level. After the construction began, one store owner
managed successfully to sue CLCO and TransLink for damages,
alleging that construction of the Canada Line ruined her business
and caused her a financial loss of about $1 million (see *Heyes v.
City of Vancouver* 2009 BCSC 651). However, this ruling was over-
turned on appeal (*Susan Heyes Inc. (Hazel & Co.) v. South Coast BC
Transportation Authority* 2011 BCCA 77), and further appeal was
refused by the Supreme Court of Canada in 2011 (Ivens 2011).

Figure 4.5   Timeline of events: The Canada Line

September 2000	Evaluation of Richmond-to-Vancouver rapid transit begins
September 2002	RAV Project Management Ltd. (RAVCO) created
November 2002	Request for Expressions of Interest for P3 involvement in a Richmond-to-Vancouver rapid transit project released; 10 submissions received
February 2003	Project definition completed
May 2003	Vancouver City Council votes in favour of the Canada Line but requests that TransLink not pursue a P3 arrangement
May 2003	Metro Vancouver votes to publicly oppose a P3 option for the Canada Line
May 2003	TransLink votes in favour of P3 for the Canada Line
January 2004	Request for Proposals for P3 involvement sent to 4 contenders identified from the Request for Expressions of Interest; 3 submissions received
May 2004	TransLink board of directors votes to discontinue the Canada Line project
June 2004	TransLink board of directors votes to discontinue the Canada Line project a second time
July 2004	Best and Final Offer invitations sent to two proponent teams who responded to the Request for Proposals
December 2004	TransLink board of directors votes to continue the Canada Line project
July 2005	Concession agreement signed with InTransit BC
December 2005	Construction begins
February 2006	RAVCO changes its name to Canada Line Rapid Transit Inc. (CLCO)
November 2007	TransLink's board of directors restructured
August 2009	Canada Line opens for service

A timeline of major events related to the Canada Line is provided in Figure 4.5.

THE SYDNEY AIRPORT RAIL LINK

In Sydney, a rail connection between the city's Central Business District and the international airport had been discussed since the 1950s (Jones 2000, 14). However, infrastructure development stalled in Australia in the 1970s and 1980s (Cardew 2003), and by the time the Sydney Airport Link was opened in May of 2000, it represented the first major extension to Sydney's rail network since the East Hills Line was completed in 1976 (Scardilli 2000).

The Sydney Airport Rail Link (also previously known as the New Southern Railway) is a ten-kilometre tunnel connecting Kingsford Smith Airport to Sydney's Central Business District. It comprises four independent stations and a fifth interchange station, and was constructed using a mix of bored tunnel and cut and cover methods. The Airport Link should be considered a technical achievement, as it was, at the time, the largest tunnel ever bored by tunnel boring machine in Australia (Jones 2000, 67).

The Sydney Airport Link project had several objectives. In addition to providing a direct rail connection between the airport and the city, the Airport Link allows trains originating from suburban stations on the Inner West and South Line to bypass the congested rail corridor at Central Station. This increased capacity for the rail network is often cited as being as important a motivator for the Airport Link as the actual connection to the airport (e.g., Kinhill Engineers 1994). Several subjects interviewed for this study, from both the private and public sectors, commented that achieving the benefits of increased capacity at Central was a primary objective of the plan for an Airport Link.

In addition, urban development has been a publicly stated objective of the Airport Link from the project's inception. The area through which the majority of the line was built had very little residential and retail commercial capacity in 1990; it was mostly home to industrial development and underdeveloped brownfield land. Planning documents identified redevelopment of these areas (aptly referred to as Sydney's "central industrial area") as a priority for the Airport Link project (New South Wales 1993, 40; Kinhill Engineers 1994; New South Wales 1994). Politicians in the state legislature frequently made reference to urban development goals as well: Bruce Baird, then minister of transport, argued that the Airport Link "would revitalise that area in terms of opportunities for medium-density housing" (Baird 1992b, 7511). One interview subject recalled that the name "Green Square," which was originally intended for one of the Airport Link's stations but now also applies to the neighbourhood in which the station is located, was invented to make the area enticing to families who might want to

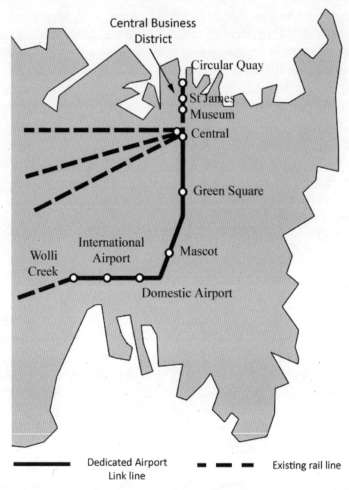

Central Business District

Circular Quay

St James

Museum

Central

Green Square

International Airport

Mascot

Wolli Creek

Domestic Airport

━━━━ Dedicated Airport Link line   ▬ ▬ ▬ Existing rail line

Figure 4.6 Route of Sydney's Airport Link

live there. By all accounts, then, one goal of the project was to allow improved public transportation to stimulate residential development along the Airport Link's route. A map of the route of the Airport Link is given in Figure 4.6.

Proposals for the Airport Link were subject to significant public dialogue. Announcements from the state government about progress in planning for the rail connection to the airport were frequent in popular media for several years before the P3 contract was finalized. A public debate took place on the choice of heavy rail versus light rail modes of service delivery, with the government favouring heavy rail despite resistance from a vocal group of light rail advocates (e.g., Baird 1991; Horrigan 1991). Community groups were enlisted for support, including the Wolli Creek Preservation Society (Jones 2000, 20) – a group that successfully lobbied for changes to the design of the M5 east freeway and whose members were later involved in a successful legal challenge to a toll road P3 in Sydney that set a precedent for Australian constitutional law (see *Truth About Motorways v. Macquarie* [2000] HCA 11).

In addition to public dialogue, the state government attempted to create an intergovernmental collaboration by requesting funds from the federal department of transport, but was ultimately unsuccessful. Because the federal and state governments were under different party banners at that time, it may have been that partisan politics, both on the part of the state and the federal government, contributed to the Australian federal government's refusal to contribute to the Airport Link project. This is certainly suggested by comments delivered in the state's Legislative Assembly (see Humpherson 1994, 179, for example). This inability of the state government to form any kind of association with Canberra for support for the Airport Link is symptomatic of the New South Wales state government's failure to promote inter-organizational networks surrounding the project. This subject will be discussed in more detail in the next chapter.

The Airport Link project began in 1989, when an Australian development company called CRI first brought an unsolicited offer to the state government to connect the airport to the city by means of existing freight rail lines (Moore 1990; Scardilli 2000). Shortly after this, the state government approached Transfield, a larger development company also based in Sydney, to see if they could provide an alternative offer, which they did. It was quickly decided that CRI's proposal was too limited as it failed to solve the Central Station congestion problem, and that the Transfield proposal had too wide a scope as it intended to construct a new tunnel from the airport straight through the Central Business District and then under the harbour all the way to North Sydney (Larriera 1991). In both cases, the proposals required considerable public sector funding, which was anathema to the state government as they had previously suggested publicly that the Airport Link could be built entirely with private finance (Lewis 1990). The state premier at the time, Nick Greiner, contacted the two companies and suggested that they collaborate on a compromise offer; this later proved to be a minor irritant to all parties involved, as the New South Wales Independent Commission Against Corruption (ICAC) initiated an investigation into impropriety in the tendering process that delayed the Airport Link project by about a year.

Fortunately for the Airport Link and for everyone involved, the premier and the government were eventually exonerated after a report by a mediator recommended they continue with the project as planned. Ironically, although the anti-corruption investigation was intended to protect transparency and accountability within government, the Independent Commission Against Corruption refused to release the mediator's final report to me upon request under the state's Government Information (Public Access) Act. An account of the incident reported in Jones (2000, 21–2) leaves many questions unanswered, such as why mediation was required, and also why the mediator (former New South Wales Supreme Court chief justice Sir Laurence Street) was able to conclude that the negotiations between the state government and the private sector to develop the Airport Link ought to continue as intended. This opacity, combined with comments from several interview subjects who stated that there was no official tendering process whatsoever, suggests the absence of a formal, accountable, private sector competition for the P3 contract.

In the end, CRI dropped out of the project and Transfield partnered with French construction giant Bouygues, at Transfield's invitation, to form the Airport Link Company, which was a special purpose vehicle incorporated solely for the Sydney Airport Link Project. Transfield and Bouygues each invested $8 million in equity and $16 million through the sale of corporate bonds, for a total of about $48 million; they also provided a further $313 million in finance through National Australia Bank (RailCorp 2005, 5). The state government of New South Wales was required to provide $940 million for the tracks and tunnels and for the interchange station at Wolli Creek (Morris 1995b; 1996a), which instigated much partisan posturing in the state legislature as the government had previously promised no public funding for the project whatsoever. These figures are summarized in Figure 4.7.

Figure 4.7 Capital funding contributions for Canada Line and Airport Link

		Canada Line		Airport Link	
		2014 Canadian dollars (millions)	% of Total capital	2014 Canadian dollars (millions)	% of Total capital
PUBLIC SECTOR	Federal government	517	19.3	0	0.0
	Provincial/state government	470	17.6	940	72.3
	Municipal governments	33	1.2	0	0.0
	Transportation authority	464	17.3	0	0.0
	Total public sector	1,484	55.5	940	72.3
PRIVATE SECTOR	Partner 1 (equity)	46	1.7	8.35	0.6
	Partner 2 (equity)	46	1.7	8.35	0.6
	Partner 3 (equity)	46	1.7	0	0.0
	Subordinated debt (corporate bonds)	0	0.0	31	2.4
	Bank loans	688	25.7	313	24.1
	Total private sector	826	30.9	360.7	27.7
OTHER	Airport authority	365	13.6	0	0.0
	Total	2,675	100.0	1,300.7	100.0

The partnership agreement for the Airport Link was signed between the Airport Link Company and a state-level government corporation called RailCorp[4] that was in charge of rail operations for all of New South Wales. RailCorp would own the tracks and tunnels, and service on the line would be provided by RailCorp's own trains through their local subsidiary. The Airport Link Company would own and operate the four independent stations for thirty years after they opened for service, after which time the entire asset would be transferred back to RailCorp. The Airport Link Company contracted the construction of the stations and the tunnels, as well as the construction of the interchange station at Wolli Creek, to the Transfield/Bouygues Joint Venture (RailCorp 2005). Shortly after construction was completed, Bouygues asked to be released from the agreement, and Transfield purchased their share of the Airport Link Company for an undisclosed amount. An organizational chart for the Sydney Airport Link is shown in Figure 4.8.

From the beginning, the plan was to repay the private sector's investment through premium fares charged directly to the Airport Link's passengers. Every iteration of the proposal included a plan for extra charges to passengers (e.g., Larriera 1991; Coultan 1992b). Since the service opened in 2000, passengers at the two airport stations have been paying both the regular urban rail fare and an additional "station access fee." As of 2015, the station access fee was in the range of $13 – over 300 per cent of the price of a comparable trip on the rest of the rail system – above the regular fare com-

4 The public agency responsible for urban transport in New South Wales has been restructured and renamed several times since the Sydney Airport Link was first devised. At the time that the original contract was signed, it was known as the State Rail Authority. In 2005, when the revised contract was signed following the legal dispute, it was called RailCorp. As of 2013, authority for rail services rests with Transport for New South Wales. Likewise, the urban rail operator in Sydney was called CityRail until 2013, but since 2013 has been called Sydney Trains. This frequent restructuring of public agencies is typical of the transport industry in New South Wales and will be discussed further in later chapters.

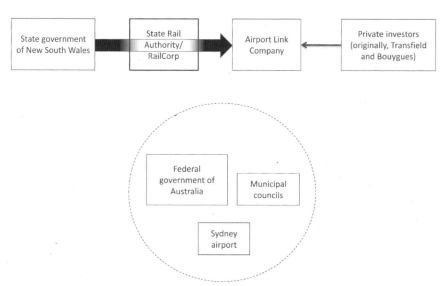

Figure 4.8 Organizational chart of the Sydney Airport Link

ponent. These high extra fares have been a sticking point for all parties and stakeholders since the Airport Link opened (see Booz and Co. 2010 for example); however, they are the only form of revenue assigned to the private sector through the P3 contract. Since 2011, the station access fees for the two non-airport suburban stations have been subsidized by the state government for all passengers, which very quickly resulted in a rise in patronage at those stations by 50–70 per cent (Saulwick 2011b).

Original patronage estimates for the Airport Link put daily ridership at 46,000 passengers per day, with a forecast rise to 65,000 daily passengers by 2013 (Kinhill Engineers 1994, 1–3). These estimates were proven to be significantly optimistic after service began: after three months, the Airport Link averaged only 10,500 daily riders (Wainwright 2000a). In November 2011, after eleven years in operation, Airport Link Company recorded its highest ever ridership levels at about 30,000 passengers per day (while public statements regarding patronage have not been made since 2005, this information was provided to me personally by an interview respondent familiar with the Airport Link Company). The Airport Link's patronage has improved substantially, but still has not even come close to meeting the original estimates.

Since ridership was so poor, and since fare surcharges were its only source of revenue, the Airport Link Company defaulted on a loan payment to National Australia Bank in November 2000 – only six months after it began operating (Wainwright 2000d). After Transfield (by then the sole parent company of Airport Link) refused to cover the payments, the bank foreclosed on the loan and appointed receivers, who later sold the company to Westpac, another Australian bank. Several interview subjects commented that the bank made a considerable profit on this sale, indicating that although ridership numbers were still nowhere near their original estimates at the time of sale, there were investors who believed the system would eventually be profitable.

These financial troubles of the Airport Link incited a bitter dispute between the state government and the Airport Link Company that took five years to resolve. The Airport Link Company argued that RailCorp had allowed service on the line to sink to a level below the minimum acceptable standards as set out in the P3 contract, and that this had significantly deterred potential customers from using the line. These standards included the number of trains passing through the Airport Link stations each day, how closely the trains kept to their schedule, how clean the trains were, and how new the equipment was. In addition, the Airport Link Company contended that RailCorp had not adequately advertised or promoted the Airport Link, and that this refusal to provide in-kind support contributed to the low ridership levels. Some of my interview respondents also suggested that labour union leaders, opposed to the P3 structure of the Airport Link which they saw as a product of anti-labour ideology, willfully sabotaged the smooth functioning of the Airport Link stations through theft of safety equipment and other activities. RailCorp and the state government, for their part, maintained consistently that the high fares for Airport Link – set by the Airport Link Company through the station access fees – were the sole cause of low ridership.

Both parties must have been reluctant to take the matter to court, because although it was not finally resolved until 2005, the dispute was settled without judicial intervention and without nationalization of the Airport Link by the state. A new financial agreement was crafted in which the Airport Link Company would continue to set and collect station access fees, but the structure of the revenue-sharing arrangement was altered so that the private partners would receive an additional $151 million over the course of the concession. This compromise had the benefit of avoiding a direct compensation payment from the public sector to the Airport Link Company, which would have had immense political consequences for the state government. In addition, increased revenue potential for the private sector had the effect of improving the financial value of the Airport Link Company, which is a benefit to the Airport Link Company and its investors.

The matter is now considered settled and my interview respondents from both the public and private sectors reported that the Airport Link Company currently enjoys a professional and amicable relationship with the state government. As of 2015, the station access fees were still being charged directly to customers at the domestic and international airport stations, although several interview subjects appeared quite confident that the state government would eventually subsidize the fees for all passengers at these stations as well. In fact, the upper chamber of the New South Wales Parliament, the Legislative Council, held an inquiry on the public subsidy of the station access fees at the airport stations that reported in 2014 (New South Wales 2014). A timeline of major events for the Sydney Airport Link is given in Figure 4.9.

COMPARING SUCCESS AND FAILURE

In chapter 3, governance failure was defined as a failure of a market-government collaboration to achieve specific policy objectives, within a normative framework justified by the policy's distributional outcomes. In the Sydney case, partnership with the private sector did not achieve the project's publicly stated policy objectives; in fact, in addition to the failure to achieve the intended goals of the project, the Sydney Airport Link P3 resulted in unstable antagonism between the public and private partners, as well as negative distributional outcomes for residents of the Greater Sydney area and taxpayers in New South Wales in general.

Figure 4.9   Timeline of Events: The Sydney Airport Link

1989	CRI proposes airport rail link on existing rail connections
November 1991	New South Wales government asks Transfield and CRI to explore options to collaborate
November 1991	New South Wales government announces, for the first time, that there would be public funding available for the Airport Link project
March 1992	Heads of Agreement signed between Transfield, CRI, the Department of Transport, and State Rail Authority to develop the Airport Link
June 1992	Nick Greiner, premier of New South Wales, resigns
October 1992	Feasibility study completed, but not released to the public for reasons of commercial confidentiality
February 1994	After several months of investigation, the Independent Commission Against Corruption (ICAC) recommends cancelling the project and starting again with a new competitive tender process; private investors threaten to sue the government
July 1994	Federal government announces it will not be contributing funding to the Airport Link project
July 1994	ICAC decides to allow the Airport Link project to continue
February 1995	Original P3 contract signed
March 1995	Liberal-National coalition loses state election; Labor comes to power
August 1995	Construction on Airport Link begins
May 2000	Sydney Airport Link opens for service
November 2000	Airport Link Company defaults on payments to its creditors, goes into receivership; receivers initiate legal action against the state government
October 2005	Legal conflict between the state government and the Airport Link's private investors settled
November 2005	Airport Link's renegotiated P3 Contract is signed
March 2011	New South Wales government begins subsidizing the station access fees at non-airport stations

As described above, the Airport Link had three main objectives: to provide a transit connection between Sydney's central business district and the airport, to relieve congestion at the Central Station rail junction, and to stimulate urban development in Sydney's southern industrial suburbs. As evidenced by the extremely low ridership levels through much of its lifespan, the Sydney Airport Link has not been a popular transit option for commuting between downtown and the airport. It has not been useful to society, because it is so expensive that it has deterred potential riders – for groups of people travelling together, taxis have at times been more economical than riding the Airport Link (Knight 2000). In addition, this public transit option has been burdensome to the airport's 16,000 employees, who received no discount and would have had to pay full price on the Airport Link if they chose to use transit to get to work (Booz and Co. 2010). This has been especially onerous since the Airport Link concession agreement required the government to cut bus service to the airport (Saulwick 2011c).

As for the other two objectives of the project, although the Airport Link's tunnel does provide for increased capacity in the Central Station area of the urban rail network, this part of the infrastructure was entirely paid for by the public sector. The final P3 agreement delegated responsibility for the stations to Transfield (Railcorp 2005), but responsibility for the tunnels was always in the hands of the government. And land development along the route has been slow (Cummins 2006). This is an expected outcome of the low patronage experienced by the system. In short, the Sydney Airport Link P3 did not achieve two of its three main policy objectives at all, and one of them – increased capacity for the rail network – was achieved in spite of the partnership, not because of it.

The public and private sector partners have consistently blamed each other for the fact that patronage on the Airport Link has been well below initial estimates for every year that it has been in service, with the private partners pointing to poor quality service and bad advertising in the early days of operation and with the state government arguing that the private surcharges were too high. The government or the rail authority could have offered to improve service, they could have integrated the Airport Link's marketing strategy with publicity for the rest of the urban rail network, and they could have offered to subsidize fares on a temporary basis or provide other incentives to promote ridership. The private sector could have reduced its short-term profit projections in order to allow for lower fares that would have encouraged more riders. However, these and other similar solutions would have required better collaboration between the public sector and private sector partners. This collaboration did not happen.

Once the Airport Link Company was declared insolvent, the government could have purchased the assets for a price that was only slightly higher than the capital investment provided by the private sector in the first place, according to several of my interview respondents. Having done so, fares on the Airport Link could have been set at the same level as the rest of the urban rail system. However, this would have required the state government to negotiate settlements with the private sector partner regarding the value of the assets, the transfer of ownership, and the transition to service integration with the rest of the publicly run system. This would have represented a level of engagement and cooperation with the private partner that the state government was clearly not willing to provide. The state was also not willing to acquire responsibility for the assets or the service at the Airport Link stations, presumably because this would have encouraged a public perception that it was accepting responsibility for the financial and ridership failure of the system.

Instead, the state government's approach was to decline to participate with the private partners in resolving the patronage problems, and to allow the bank to foreclose on the Airport Link Company's debt. This event resulted in legal action from National Australia Bank, which then forced the state government into a position where it had no choice but to negotiate with the bank's receivers for a new P3 concession agreement. While the state's strategy up to this point had been to avoid engaging with the private sector, the bankruptcy of the Airport Link company placed it in a position where it was forced to negotiate, because of the legal partnership requirements stipulated by the P3 contract. According to interview subjects, whereas the struggling Airport Link Company had been in a desperate situation and was willing to negotiate, the bank was patient, had little to lose, and had deeper pockets, which meant that it would strike immediately with legal action and could afford to wait for the most favourable outcome. This course of action resulted in financial penalties for the public sector partners.

The Airport Link therefore qualifies as a governance failure. Because the partners were not able to collaborate sustainably, the governance arrangement did not realize its public service objectives of providing a useful rail transit option from Sydney's central business district to the airport and encouraging urban development in some of Sydney's underdeveloped industrial suburbs. Although the project did increase rail capacity on the urban rail network, this was an achievement of the public sector and not of the partnership.

The Canada Line, by contrast, and despite considerable controversy, accomplished all of its stated policy objectives and maintained productive cooperation between the public and private sector partners throughout its development and into its operating period. The line was constructed as designed; it was completed on time and on budget (Yaffe 2010); it was in use during the Olympics; it was partially financed and is operated by the private sector; and, since it has met and surpassed all ridership forecasts (Hager 2011), the Canada Line has achieved its functional objective as a major component of Vancouver's urban rail network. In addition, impending housing and commercial construction along the Canada Line's route means that the government's urban development objectives will soon begin to be realized as well (Sinoski 2010). And while it is arguable that construction of the Canada Line produced unacceptable disruption to business owners and residents along the construction route, it would be difficult to conclude that this resulted in a governance failure, because (a) the system remains popular as evidenced by high ridership levels, and (b) a business owner who claimed her business was destroyed by Canada Line construction did not win her high-profile lawsuit, meaning that the courts have proclaimed the construction techniques of the Canada Line to be acceptable and legitimate. In other words, the verdict in the courts as well as in the court of popular opinion (attestable through ridership levels and opinion polls) appears to be that the Canada Line P3 can be normatively justified. Since it achieved its stated objectives and did so within the bounds of publicly accepted norms, the Canada Line cannot be considered a governance failure.

Although the Canada Line and the Sydney Airport Link are exceedingly similar cases, they do have a number of physical and operational differences that need to be addressed. Most prominently, the Sydney Airport Link uses a premium fare system to charge users extra fares directly. Conversely, when it opened, the Canada Line charged most users the same fares as they would have been charged for a similar trip on the rest of the system. The notable exception to this rule would be trips that began and ended entirely on the airport arm of the system, which were free, and cash fares (as opposed to pre-purchased tickets or passes) that originated at the airport and terminated beyond the airport arm, which incurred a $5 surcharge.[5] This surcharge was intended to act exactly like the station access fees in the Sydney case: it has been exclusively returned to the private partner as a revenue-generating device. However, the key difference between the two extra charges results from the fact that in Sydney it is the private operator who sets the price, which means it is virtually unlimited. In Vancouver, the public sector (TransLink, formerly subject to oversight from an independent regulatory commission) sets all prices, including the airport premium, and this extra charge is further limited by the fact that the public sector transportation authority is prohibited from profiting by it (YVR 2005). High fares on the Sydney Airport Link undoubtedly contributed to lower patronage levels, so the arrangement that allowed the private sector to set the station access fees is a crucial factor in understanding how governance failure occurred in the Sydney case.

In addition, there were some jurisdictional differences that created slightly different political conditions in Sydney from those under which the Canada Line was conceived. For one thing, the local transportation authorities in the two cases had very different political mandates (although highly similar operational functions). TransLink in Vancouver is a mainly autonomous organization that is somewhat protected from political intervention. It sets its own priorities and long-term strategic

5 The introduction of an electronic fare card was implemented in 2015, but it did not immediately change the basic structure of fees related to the Canada Line.

planning, controls its own budget, and enjoys some independence in selecting its executives (though not its board of directors). It is, of course, ultimately a statutory creation of the province and is therefore subject in the end to the will of the provincial government. The provincial government also has legislative control over TransLink's revenue sources, which allows it to use less coercive measures to negotiate with the organization, as it did when it cancelled the parking stall tax in 2004 (Steffenhagen 2004) or when it announced the P3 financial architecture of the Canada Line when that project began. In Sydney, the rail authority was always operationally independent, but over the last fifteen years it has been subject to multiple restructuring and rebranding efforts by the state government. The state government has also replaced the transportation authority's executive officers, especially the chief executive, on numerous occasions. Individuals interviewed for this research indicated overwhelmingly that during the Airport Link project's development the transportation authority was entirely dependent on the state government for direction. This, again, is symptomatic of the New South Wales state government's general inability to sustain the kind of inter-organizational network that might have prevented a governance failure.

And lastly, the Sydney Airport Link was built through mainly industrial areas, in which the state was intending to promote urban development (Kinhill Engineers 1994). Urban development has been a stated goal of the Canada Line and its construction as well (see, for example, RAV Project Management Ltd. 2005b, 6), but the fact remains that many areas in which the Canada Line construction took place – such as the downtown core, the mixed-use residential and commercial area known as Cambie Village, and the shopping district in the city of Richmond – were at a more advanced stage of development than those of the Sydney Airport Link. This allowed for disturbance to residents and business owners in the Vancouver case that was not very likely to occur in Sydney. However, even though the conflict that occurred in Vancouver over construction-related disruption to local businesses was unique to that case, the way in which it was handled by the project management firm known as CLCO provides an informative example of conflict mitigation to prevent governance failure. This would not have been possible for the Sydney project and its participants.

PREVIOUS RESEARCH

Other commentators have reviewed both the Canada Line and the Sydney Airport Link. In the case of the Canada Line, in addition to technical articles on construction techniques, there have been a number of academic pieces that have appeared since it was announced. Many of these have only made passing commentary about the P3 aspect of the project (e.g., Hatzopoulou and Miller 2007; Vining and Boardman 2008) or have concentrated on very specific issues like racial discrimination among construction workers (Shantz 2011). The few studies that have focused on the organizational structure of the Canada Line have made important contributions to our understanding of the governance of P3s. However, the story is still incomplete as it has been related to date.

Siemiatycki (2006; 2007) and Hutton (2012) both argue that the use of a P3 arrangement for the design, procurement, and operation of the Canada Line has and will continue to increase conflict, both between the project's partners and between the government and the general public. As Siemiatycki (2006) sees it, the P3 arrangement presents an inherent contradiction: P3s should enhance responsible governance practices by encouraging competition between non-political private sector actors; however, private sector competition requires trade secrecy, which undermines accountability and transparency. Although commercial confidentiality is considered necessary for allowing P3s to operate as intended, Siemiatycki (2007) finds that confidentiality privileges can be abused. In the case of the Canada Line, according to Siemiatycki, this resulted in decreased legitimacy through an exaggeration of the financial benefits and probability of success (both financial and ridership) of the line, and led to feelings of disenfranchisement among stakeholders.

Hutton (2012) argues that the Canada Line project was from the beginning a tenuous coalition of unwilling partners, each jockeying for position in an arena where the provincial government maintains a stranglehold on decision-making capability. The creation of the project management corporation CLCO is, therefore, an institutionalization of this conflict, which according to Hutton manifested itself most palpably in the ordeal that occurred early in the project as the city of Vancouver, TransLink, and Metro Vancouver alternatingly voted for and against approval of the Canada Line. For Hutton, the traditional powers of the provincial government and its constitutional superiority over local authorities mean that contractual arrangements like P3s, where provincial authority is less explicit and where government organizations at different political levels are forced to maintain the appearance of cooperation, will amplify conflict between these actors.

Other authors have claimed that the P3 aspect of the Canada Line did not increase conflict, either between P3 partners or between government and the general public. Regeczi (2008), in a study comparing P3 and non-P3 infrastructure in Canada and Hungary, finds that avenues of communication between network participants in P3s are not necessarily obstructed. What's more, Regeczi argues that this free-flowing communication, along with the fact that the government partner in a P3 can maintain a central position in the network, means that accountability, transparency, and legitimacy can be preserved in P3s and that this was the case for the Canada Line.

Cohn (2008) takes the middle ground. He contends that conflict was mitigated in the case of the Canada Line by the fact that much of the political aspect of the project was removed. This is because the use of a P3 arrangement changes the rules of the game, by delegating more power to apolitical, technically expert, bureaucrats. For the development of the Canada Line, according to Cohn, the Liberal government of British Columbia intentionally selected a P3 arrangement in order to push a capital-heavy infrastructure building agenda at the same time as they intended to develop a low tax, low spending, small government image. While the political executive maintained control as it ultimately decided which projects to procure as a P3 and which not to, the power of the bureaucracy was magnified by the contractual nature of P3s – combined with a deliberate framing of policy decisions as a choice between having a P3 project or not having a project at all. By redirecting decisions to the bureaucracy in this way, Cohn argues that the political level could be removed from the narrative of the development of the Canada Line; however, it also reduced the legitimacy of the project as unelected technocrats were given decision-making capabilities that they could exercise beyond the reach of public discourse.

As I will show in the next three chapters, all of these existing analyses are incomplete. For one thing, Siemiatycki's focus on a small group of disgruntled business owners and Hutton's assessment of CLCO as an institutionalization of conflict are narrow views that do not capture the bigger picture of the network of interaction between participants in the Canada Line project. An alternative to these two viewpoints, based on the same observations, would be that the network of actors created for the Canada Line was a complex and expertly managed organization of interaction that effectively suppressed conflict and delivered a product that has been and continues to be extremely popular. This is especially evident when the Canada Line is compared to a similar project that experienced governance failure, such as the Sydney Airport Link, in which conflict was unquestionable and legitimacy was widely disputed. In fact the participants in the Canada Line, and especially the public sector partners that Siemiatycki and Hutton are so critical of, managed to mitigate participant conflict that could have proven disastrous. This is evidenced by the outcomes in the case of the Airport Link.

Secondly, Regeczi's analysis that the Canada Line did not reduce channels of communication, and therefore overall accountability and legitimacy, is also incomplete because he does not take into consideration the agency of the public sector actors who endeavoured to make this possible. As with Siemiatycki's and Hutton's arguments, Regeczi lacks the comparison between the Canada Line and a similar case that experienced governance failure, which would allow him to examine the factors that enabled effective communication and network interaction in the case of the Canada Line.

And thirdly, Cohn's analysis, while astute, suffers from the same problem: he sees the removal of the political level as an unfortunate loss of legitimacy, whereas by comparison to a case like the Sydney Airport Link it becomes clear that this is likely what prevented the Canada Line from descending into a scenario of governance failure.

Like the Canada Line, there is only a small selection of academic scholarship available regarding the Sydney Airport Link. Several reports consider the Airport Link in passing while commenting on greater political issues surrounding the use of P3s in Australia (e.g., Searle 1999; Cardew 2003; Watson 2003). Lilley and de Giorgio (2004) review the Airport Link case and conclude that "failure" was due to incorrect ridership forecasts and poor contract design, but they do not elaborate on how these errors came to be committed or how the dynamics of interaction between the partner organizations may have contributed to outcomes. Ng and Loosemore (2007) present the Airport Link as a case study in risk management, but again they do not consider the internal mechanisms of the partnership arrangement.

Early on, before the contract was officially signed, Walker (1994) published an in-depth analysis of the financial arrangement of the Airport Link. This report, which was widely cited in the news media at the time (see Morris 1994b for example), concluded that the deal unfairly disadvantaged the public sector. However, Walker did not have access to the official contract details and was working solely with a preliminary feasibility study. In addition, many of my interview respondents, from both the public and the private sector, commented that Walker's analysis was incorrect. This is corroborated by the fact that the original private sector partners did not pocket the fantastic profits at the financial expense of the government and taxpayers that Walker's study predicted they would.

In short, what is lacking from the existing body of academic literature is a study that analyzes the networked interactions in a public-private partnership to try to determine if certain relationships or mechanisms can become causal factors for governance failure. The best way to do this would be to compare a P3 project that resulted in a governance failure with a similar project that did not, thereby isolating the important causal factors as best as possible. To date, this has not yet been done. In the next three chapters, I begin to fill this gap by presenting three methods of strategic policy leadership that were used by the public sector in the case of the

Canada Line to prevent governance failure. These methods were not employed in the case of the Sydney Airport Link and, as will be seen presently, this contributed to the divergent outcomes in the two cases.

CONCLUSION

Superficially, the difference between the Canada Line and the Sydney Airport Link appears to be fairly simple: the Airport Link had a faulty initial ridership estimate, which supported a flawed business model based on an expensive premium surcharge. The high cost of the system deterred customers and led to bankruptcy. The Canada Line project was luckier with its patronage estimates, and decision makers in British Columbia chose a safer business model in which the transit authority sets the price, so the fares were much lower. From this perspective, success or failure is related to the price of the system and the decisions that led to setting that price.

However, this is a proximate answer, not an ultimate one. Explaining failure in terms of high station access fees does not answer fundamental questions about the Airport Link saga, such as why this fee structure was adopted in the first place. Why was the Airport Link P3 allowed to be designed so badly? Why, with government planners, private sector experts in transportation systems, and supervision from political decision makers, was a flawed business model ever adopted? And even if price were the fundamental cause of failure, it alone would not explain why low ridership resulted in an extended legal battle. Why was conflict between the partners in this case not resolved quickly and amicably? Why didn't conflict in the case of the Canada Line – of which there was no shortage – result in a similar disruption of the project?

These questions cannot be answered away with the premiums charged to passengers on the Sydney Airport Link. In fact, the story is substantially more complicated. The tactics employed by the state in the case of the Canada Line helped prevent its failure, and these similar tactics were absent in the Sydney Airport Link – an absence that contributed to failure in that case. As will be seen in the following chapters, the governance of public-private partnerships requires a strategic, activist state that is mindful of its non-state actors. States that attempt to engage in P3s while ignoring important network participants – many of whom have substantial responsibility for public policy decision making – run the risk that negative outcomes could spiral into failure.

5

Supporting and Managing Policy Networks

In chapter 3, I argued that in the present climate, networks are crucial to the formulation and implementation of public policy. This is because, in the thirty or so years since alternative governance arrangements have grown in use and popularity, much responsibility for policy has already been delegated to independent actors, such as autonomous public sector organizations, state-owned corporations, and private sector entities. Many of these actors – such as independent regulators, municipal councils, chambers of commerce, and professional oversight bodies (the Law Society, for example) – have partial responsibility for, or influence in, areas that affect greater policy decisions. The combined output of these organizations results in network decision making, which is now an essential part of modern governance.

Also in chapter 3, I argued that because of the inherent anarchy of policy networks, and because of the state's ultimate responsibility to its citizenry, the state must take an active role in supporting and managing networks. I further argued more specifically that leadership on the part of the government is essential to successful network governance.

In this chapter, I will apply these claims to the public-private partnerships of the Canada Line and the Sydney Airport Link. By comparing how the state government in New South Wales and the provincial government in British Columbia interacted with network participants in these two cases, I will show that in the case of the Canada Line, the government ensured the smooth functioning of the P3 by making itself a recognized and respected network authority, while simultaneously supporting the power and responsibility of appropriate network participants. In Sydney, the Airport Link P3 failed in part because the government was unable or unwilling to do the same. In British Columbia, unlike in New South Wales, the government recognized that network decision making is different than hierarchical single-authority decision making; by acting mainly through authoritative posturing, indirect manipulation, and careful delegation of responsibility, it was able to achieve its intended objectives.

A FUNCTIONING POLICY NETWORK
FOR THE CANADA LINE

From the beginning, the government of British Columbia strived to achieve a cohesive and functional policy network for the development of the Canada Line. Numerous efforts on the part of the political executive, as well as those of decision makers at TransLink (and later, CLCO), worked to ensure the participation of relevant network actors, and supported communication and cooperation between them.

In 2002, the political executive assembled representatives of all of the public sector entities that would have an interest in participating in a rapid transit extension to Vancouver International Airport and to the suburb of Richmond, and created a steering committee to oversee the project definition phase. This steering committee included the CEO and the director of planning of TransLink, as well as representatives from the provincial Ministry of Transportation, the federal government's Western Economic Diversification branch, the federal Ministry of Transportation (Transport Canada), Metro Vancouver, the Vancouver Port Authority, the City of Vancouver and the City of Richmond, and Vancouver International Airport (RAV Project Management Ltd. 2003, 28). Well before the private sector was ever engaged, the relevant public sector organizations in British Columbia's transportation policy network were already interacting and communicating on a united vision for the project.

Next, the provincial government negotiated with the federal government to secure federal-level funding for the project, and once that funding was secured, then-premier Gordon Campbell lobbied the federal government directly (and persistently, over two years) to increase its financial commitment to the project from $345 million to $517 million (O'Neill 2004). In the end the federal government was the single biggest funding contributor for the project (hence the name "Canada Line," which was applied at the federal government's request). While the ruling party in British Columbia and in Ottawa at the time were both called the Liberals, the two parties are not organizationally or politically connected, and the provincial government's efforts to secure federal funding should be viewed as the result of effective negotiation.

Further, the decision makers for the Canada Line project exhibited exceptional outreach to the general public at every stage of the project's development. Four major rounds of public consultation occurred: during the project definition phase in 2003, during the pre-design phase in 2003-04, and twice during the design phase in 2005 (RAV Project Management Ltd. 2005c). Representatives from local advocacy groups were frequently directly invited to participate in events, and the Canada Line's project managers participated in other groups' events: in one example, CLCO sent its own representatives to open meetings held by the Environmental Youth Alliance, a local non-profit community sustainability group (Cornerstone Planning 2003; InTransit BC 2006). In addition, there was a separate public consultation for the airport arm of the project in 2005, as well as further public outreach conducted as part of the private partner's "Best and Final Offer" bid (RAV Project Management Ltd. 2005a, Schedule 6). While these last two were not conducted by the government or its agencies, my interview subjects commented that the culture of public consultation that was adopted early on by the government, TransLink, and CLCO inspired these other organizations to follow suit.

In addition to general public consultation, the Canada Line promoted reciprocal communication with the business community. Business liaison committees were created in Vancouver and in Richmond, in which representatives from various local business improvement associations, CLCO, municipal governments, and the private sector P3 partner met to discuss strategies to support businesses disturbed by the construction of the Canada Line (Sanatani 2007). Despite the fact that some business owners were not satisfied with these efforts (culminating, as described earlier, in legal action), business associations continually praised the efforts of the Canada Line's business liaison program and denounced reports of friction between the project and the business community as "misleading" (Bellett 2007a).

In general, stakeholder input was highly valued. One interview respondent related a story of a community-based petition to change the recommended location of the Yaletown station (one of the stations located on the edge of Vancouver's downtown core): CLCO, in response to what turned out to be a substantial amount of support for this petition, invested considerable money in examining the possibility of relocating the station, going as far as to commission an engineering report and a cost-benefit analysis. After reading the results of the report, which revealed the new location to be significantly more expensive, the community relented and the station was built in the originally designated location. While the petitioners did not ultimately get their way in this example, my interview respondent claimed that the Canada Line project managers took their request "very seriously," commissioned extra reports, and held consultations to satisfy their concerns. Other interviewees commented that, as with public outreach, the multilateral cooperation that was prioritized early on by the government contributed to a culture of collaboration later in the life cycle of the project, leading to exceptionally high levels of communication between the various stakeholders, as well as lower levels of inter-organizational friction than they had seen on other projects in their experience.

Additionally, by all accounts, the involvement of the Airport Authority in the project was crucial to its success. All of my interview respondents who were familiar with the early (i.e., pre-2002) stages of the Canada Line agreed that it was unclear if the project would go ahead as a Richmond-Vancouver transit line, but as soon as the Airport Authority expressed an interest in funding an airport connector, the concept suddenly became much more viable. Interview respondents also commented that strong local political champions, like Richmond Mayor Malcolm Brodie and former Vancouver Mayor Larry Campbell, were crucial to the project becoming a reality. The fact that the province was willing to work with multiple actors (including local politicians and the airport) and to take their concerns seriously is a testament to how much

the provincial government valued the network and its participants. When asked about the involvement of the City of Vancouver, for example, many interview respondents commented that the
City was treated as a full project partner, to the extent that both the
City of Vancouver and the City of Richmond were invited to participate in the procurement phase, which was unusual for provincially led infrastructure projects. This is especially intriguing con-
sidering that the City of Vancouver provided a very small capital
contribution (around $30 million, mainly for the construction of
an extra station) and that the City of Richmond did not contribute
any capital funding at all.

In addition to fostering inter-organizational communication
and information sharing, the British Columbia provincial government allowed free expression of ideas by not directly sup-
pressing any controversy or debate surrounding the Canada Line
project. The polarized tone of the debates – in which expert opinions contradicted each other and serious conflict ensued among
elected politicians to the extent that the project was nearly cancelled – ensured that it received prominent coverage in the local
media (see Bula 2003b; Lee 2004 for example). Public statements
in this time period were often dramatic. For example, after one
particularly difficult meeting in which municipal politicians
who sat on TransLink's board of directors voted not to continue
with the project, the chair of TransLink commented that the
Canada Line "is dead now ... This is a huge lost opportunity. We
gave away a billion dollars" (Boei 2004). The provincial government did not attempt to interfere with the municipal councils or
with TransLink to silence the conflict, or to pressure them into a
more politically palatable tone, although it was within its power
to do so.

It is true that the multi-lateral institutional composition of the
Greater Vancouver metropolitan region facilitated this debate.
Then, as now, the provincial government was not the only government with jurisdiction over transportation in Vancouver. The
City of Vancouver and the City of Richmond are active players
in the local transportation policy network. Additionally, Metro
Vancouver, whose council is composed of the mayors of the
twenty-one municipalities in the metropolitan region, contributed greatly to policy decisions in this area. And the local

transit authority, TransLink, was at the time governed directly by Metro Vancouver mayors and city councillors and had its own internal policy objectives to create and achieve. So in this sense, the provincial government was constrained by other legitimate players who controlled transportation policy direction in the region to some extent.

However, this perspective is incomplete. For one, it is a well-known outcome of Canadian constitutional jurisprudence that provincial governments have complete control over cities within their jurisdictional boundaries. Some provinces have wielded this power in its ultimate capacity, creating and eliminating cities and municipal governments as they see fit. Ontario and Quebec, especially, have not shied away from this tactic even in the face of substantial public animosity (Kushner and Siegel 2003; Mévellec 2009). The relationship between Canadian provinces and their municipalities is complex and involves a host of political and administrative issues, such as the downloading of responsibility for service delivery to local governments with concurrent decreases in block funding; nonetheless, provincial control over municipal governments is widely considered politically legitimate, and municipal governments are therefore considered weak by Canadian legal and constitutional standards (Sancton 2012).[1] If the British Columbia provincial government had wanted to avoid a public debate on the Canada Line at the local level, it could easily have stifled the regional or municipal governments by threat or by direct force. Instead, it allowed the debate to carry on in full view of the local media, even to the point where the actors involved believed that the Canada Line project would be cancelled in its entirety (Boei 2004).

The provincial government aimed to promote a cohesive policy network for urban transit in Vancouver, but it did not presume to dictate policy directly or to command the various participants to

[1] The City of Vancouver is unusual in that it is governed by the Vancouver Charter, a provincial statute that delegates specific authority to Vancouver's city council for a number of policy areas. However, the Charter is legislative, not constitutional, and can be altered unilaterally by the province, as has been done on numerous occasions (e.g., Lee 1988; Skelton 2004; Lee and Rolfsen 2009).

act under specific directives. Instead, the province maintained the illusion of a hands-off approach, mainly using pressure, persuasion, exhortation, and carefully veiled threats to achieve the results it desired. For example, not only did the provincial government not stop the local-level political debate on the Canada Line, but it also categorically refused to enter the debate in its full capacity. In the provincial legislature, there is virtually no discussion of the topic before 2003, which is conspicuous as there would have been a lot of planning in the years 1999–2003 when TransLink was getting off the ground and a Richmond-Airport-Vancouver rapid transit project was becoming a real priority.

From the time it was elected in 2001, the Liberal government continually disavowed any responsibility for decision making for the Canada Line. In the legislature, Premier Campbell frequently referred to the Canada Line as a TransLink project, not a provincial government one, and definitely not an official part of the 2010 Winter Olympics bid (e.g., Campbell 2004, 11310). Kevin Falcon, the provincial minister of transportation during most of the Canada Line's development, argued that the province's role was strictly to provide funding and nothing more – and that the province was therefore not liable for any decision making, access to information, cost overruns, or negotiation with the private sector (Falcon 2005, 1283). In October 2009, after the Canada Line had opened for operations, then minister of transportation Shirley Bond told the legislature that the provincial government did not have a single full-time employee dedicated to the Canada Line, whereas it had at that point twelve full-time employees dedicated to the region's next big transit project, the Evergreen Line, which was not a P3 (Bond 2009). These sentiments were reiterated in statements that provincial politicians made to the press during this time as well: when asked to comment on a regional-level vote to discontinue development of the Canada Line project, Kevin Falcon told *The Vancouver Sun*, "It's their decision. We'll move on." (Boei 2004).

The provincial government also refused to interfere with the governance of TransLink during this time period. As mentioned previously, TransLink's board of directors was composed of mayors and councillors drawn from a weighted average of representatives from the Metro Vancouver regional city councils. According to the law that established TransLink (Greater Vancouver Transportation Authority Act 1998, s.8), the provincial government had the right to appoint three members of its own to TransLink's board as direct representatives of the province; however, from 1999 until the law was amended in 2007, these positions were never filled. It is typical of the provincial government's modus operandi with respect to the Canada Line that it never appointed provincial representatives to the regional transportation authority's board of directors – even when doing so would have ended the divisive debates that were perpetuated at this level during the development period of the project (several votes were close enough that three partisan board members could have tipped the balance).

However, in a demonstration of the province's total legislative dominance of TransLink, the provincial government amended TransLink's statutory framework in 2007, *replacing its entire board* with independent directors in a restructuring that prevents local politicians from becoming directors. The new law, the South Coast British Columbia Transportation Authority Act, decrees that eligible appointees to the board of directors must not "hold elected public office of any type" (s.170). It is extremely telling that the provincial government held this kind of legislative and coercive power over the transportation authority but decided not to use it to force a conclusion to the public debate over the Canada Line, even when it is clear from later actions that this could have produced the outcome that senior provincial politicians were looking for (i.e., immediate approval of the Canada Line in a P3 format). When it finally exercised its statutory powers to restructure the board, the provincial government did not replace any of TransLink's executives. This move ensured continuity of decision-making personnel within the organization, but still enabled the government to remove interference from local governments from the management of regional public transit. These efforts represent a masterful display of political astuteness that allowed the transit authority and the local governments to interact freely and conduct a high-profile public debate during the development of the Canada Line, while at the same time deflecting blame away from the provincial government. Once the debate had been resolved and the Canada Line contracts had been signed, the government moved swiftly to restructure the organization.

Admittedly, the majority of the provincial government's actions in fostering and managing an effective policy network occurred before the project's financial close with the private partner. After the contracts were signed, collaboration was mainly either stipulated by contract or managed independently by CLCO. However, the ease with which the project was managed by the terms of the P3 contract and by the project management activities of CLCO is a direct result of actions taken by the provincial government during the design and procurement phase to secure a functioning and effective network of participants. With a robust policy network like the one the province created and fostered, and with a recognized supreme authority in the provincial government, the project was able to stabilize, and the potential for further conflict was minimized.

MAINTAINING AUTHORITY, BUT SUBTLY

Despite its desired image of a decision-less, powerless, hands-off funding source, the provincial government did expend considerable energy in directly manipulating the policy network and the Canada Line project from its inception. Nonetheless, it did this in a more subtle manner than might have been used in previous decades where policy decisions were handed down through government hierarchies. To begin with, executives at TransLink and CLCO were selected not only as highly skilled and experienced professionals, but also as well-connected industry insiders who were personally networked with senior executives across the private sector. Many of them were experienced with P3s and sympathetic to the provincial government's position. Several of these individuals went on to work for the private sector after the completion of the Canada Line, and some were directly hired by SNC-Lavalin, the private partner in the Canada Line P3. This is indicative of their merit as professionals and technical experts, but also of their personal connections within the network. Several of my interviewees confirmed that many of the high-level figures in the Canada Line project were personally familiar with each other, as they had worked together on Vancouver's previous rail extension, the Millennium Line, or on other projects.

Second, the provincial executive made development as a P3 a strict condition of the province's funding contribution for the Canada Line. The provincial government repeatedly – but indirectly – manipulated the debate process by declaring that no provincial support would be available for any alternative technologies (such as light rail) or alternative financing structures (such as raising property taxes) and by offering to take over the project in its entirety if TransLink decided not to proceed. The provincial government also increased its contribution to allow the project to proceed as a P3 after the Best and Final Offer bid came in lower than expected (Bula and Beatty 2004).

Third, the provincial government gave Partnerships BC administrative oversight for the P3 aspect of the Canada Line's development. This is stipulated in the province's funding agreement for the Canada Line project (British Columbia 2005). However, as has been noted, this was probably just posturing, as multiple interview respondents, including several senior officials, commented that Partnerships BC's role in the Canada Line project was minimal, especially compared to its influence over other P3 projects in the province. Nonetheless, whether it exercised authority or not, Partnerships BC was technically given "watchdog" status over the P3 development process for the Canada Line, and this is another example of how the provincial government asserted its authority over the project without resorting to direct intervention. In a similar yet more blatant example, the provincial funding agreement contains a clause reminding the participating organizations that the provincial government continues to be the final legal authority over the Canada Line and can overturn any element of the project that falls within its legislative jurisdiction (British Columbia 2005, 36–7). This clause was never used, but it clearly gives the province the appearance of supreme authority.

Fourth, the province further manipulated public perceptions of the Canada Line project by making certain that the Canada Line would not be seen as an Olympics project. In addition to statements made in the legislature and to the media as discussed above, the provincial funding agreement made the relationship explicit:

"The concession agreement must stipulate that the concessionaire may not use '2010' or any Olympic mark, or link the project in any way to the 2010 Olympic games in its communications or advertising, unless separately licensed or otherwise approved in writing by the Games Committee" (British Columbia 2005, 18). These efforts ensured that all public debate regarding the Canada Line would be confined to that issue and would not allow any controversy surrounding the Olympics to have an influence.

Fifth, the provincial government actively prioritized the Canada Line over other projects, including the Evergreen Line to the northeastern suburbs and the proposed rapid transit line to the University of British Columbia – both of which were designated by TransLink and Metro Vancouver as higher priorities than the Canada Line. Despite public statements indicating otherwise, the Canada Line may have been prioritized in part because of its usefulness for the Olympics; however, my interview respondents suggested that the Canada Line was sent to the front of the queue because it was viewed as financially sustainable through high initial ridership levels, and was therefore a good candidate for a public-private partnership. Prior to 2001, all transit infrastructure had been funded entirely by the provincial government. The Canada Line was the first major public transit project to be proposed after the Liberals were elected to power in British Columbia in 2001. It is therefore likely that the Canada Line was prioritized because it provided the provincial government with a flagship project through which it could demonstrate the application of public-private partnerships (again, see Cohn 2008).

And lastly, the province created CLCO as an independent project management company with direct responsibility for the project, and gave it substantial authority over the design, procurement, and financial close of the P3. Several interview subjects from several different organizations commented that this arrangement forced TransLink to accept policy decisions it would otherwise have wanted to alter. According to interviewees, if TransLink had been solely responsible for the Canada Line, it would have managed the project very differently: more money would have been spent on station design, extra stations, access to the system, connectivity with existing infrastructure, and a variety of other items related to the public service aspect of the Canada Line during its operating period. This is because TransLink, as the organization responsible for the functionality of the Line within the larger transportation network, was more concerned about the operating period than the construction period. However, the terms of the arrangement with the other network participants (including the provincial government, the Vancouver Airport Authority, the private sector, and CLCO) compelled TransLink to compromise.

Many external actors publicly recognized the provincial government's position of authority over the Canada Line. According to one high-ranking official, the private sector consortium that was to become the Canada Line's P3 concessionaire refused to sign the concession agreement with CLCO or TransLink, even though these organizations were fully authorized to close the deal. The private sector partner insisted that the provincial government sign the document. Likewise, the second lawsuit against the Canada Line – in which the owner of a business located along the construction route sued the Canada Line and the City of Vancouver for loss of business due to construction disturbance – failed because the courts recognized the statutory authority of the government to create a nuisance in the interests of the greater common good (*Susan Heyes Inc. (Hazel & Co.) v. South Coast B.C. Transportation Authority 2011 BCCA 77*, paras 151–64). Despite its desire to be perceived as a neutral financial guarantor and nothing further, the provincial government acted, and was accordingly recognized, as a responsible and active authority over the Canada Line.

In short, the provincial government played its part in the Canada Line P3 project in precisely the way that is required in a system in which multiple independent but interconnected entities control elements of responsibility for policy decision making: the government supported information sharing, debate, and cooperation among network actors, all while positioning itself as an ultimate authority with power to step in when necessary.

THE ABSENCE OF A FUNCTIONING POLICY NETWORK IN NEW SOUTH WALES

In Sydney, the New South Wales state government did not pursue the same course of action with respect to the Sydney Airport Link as the British Columbia government did with the Canada Line.

Conversely, as will be elaborated below, throughout the design, procurement, and even into the operating phase of the Airport Link project, successive governments of New South Wales persistently ignored potential policy network participants. Furthermore, they did not foster collaboration, and attempted to manage the project alone, without regard for other actors who had a vested interest in the project and without effective displays of authoritative leadership. Although the Airport Link project was technically under the authority of RailCorp, the state government intervened throughout the course of the project's development and many of my interview subjects reported that organizational boundaries between the Ministry of Transport and RailCorp were not respected. This resulted in a poorly designed P3 contract, a financially unstable private partner, and a highly adversarial and partisan approach to the entire project that permitted a protracted and costly legal dispute to occur between the government and the private sector.

To begin with, the Sydney metropolitan region does not have any form of institutionalized collaboration among municipal councils. As a consequence, cooperation or alignment among local governments is a responsibility of the state government. In 1990, when the Sydney Airport Link project was initiated, there were more municipal governments in the region than there are now, as municipal mergers have been employed, ostensibly to improve economic and bureaucratic efficiency (Dollery et al. 2008). However, throughout the development of the Airport Link, no attempts were made to unite the interests of local councils.

In fact, several interview respondents commented that the local governments were either deliberately shut out or otherwise completely ignored. One interview subject told me that the city councils were "useless" and that there would have been no point in cooperating with them. Another interview subject claimed that the City of Sydney was very much against the premium surcharges on the Airport Link, but that their concerns fell on deaf ears; this same respondent told me that the city council of Botany Bay (the area that contains Sydney International Airport) was highly in favour of an airport link but that no one considered their support to be necessary or desirable. The message appears to be that although municipal councils seem to have voiced concerns or preferences, their input was not validated in any way by the state government, and so they were left out of the process. There is no official document or news report that provides information on any activity having to do with the Airport Link that was performed by a municipality.

Likewise, the state did not manage to get the federal government to participate in the project, either politically or financially. In all likelihood, this was due to partisan reasons: at the time that the Airport Link was under development, the New South Wales state government was a Liberal/National party coalition, while the federal government was under the Labor banner (and later, when the Airport Link was under construction and after it opened, these positions were reversed). Nevertheless, the state government's strategy was apparently not to negotiate, but rather to ask for money repeatedly from the federal minister of transport, and then to get denied several times, which they may have viewed as an effective way to exploit partisan differences to shame the federal government and build sympathy for the party in power in the state government. However, according to a reading of Hansard and news reports from that time period (see Morris 1994a for example), this tactic does not appear to have worked, as the federal government staunchly refused to get involved in the project and the New South Wales Coalition government was subsequently voted out of office at the next state election. Following this, these dynamics of non-cooperation between the state of New South Wales and the federal government continued when the state government was taken over by the Labor party and the government in Canberra had switched to Liberal.

These outcomes are not entirely surprising, as federal/state/municipal interaction is not automatic in Australia. Intergovernmental relations in Australia are highly adversarial, especially in the last twenty years in which there have been significant efforts by the federal government to centralize national policy in various areas of concurrent constitutional powers (Hollander and Patapan 2007). Although there has been some effort at increased intergovernmental cooperation since 2001, historically Australian federalism has been marked by "suspicion and hostility" (Painter 2001, 145). Even in times when party labels are in alignment, states have better chances at cooperation with each other than with the Commonwealth government (Tiernan 2008, 131). This would make federal-state collaboration much more difficult to achieve in New South Wales than federal-provincial collaboration was in British Columbia.

Nonetheless, the state government did not provide the leadership that was required in building and supporting a policy network surrounding the Sydney Airport Link P3 project. In a further example of how the government of New South Wales ignored potential network participants, the Sydney International Airport was not involved in the development of the project. One of my interview respondents observed that the airport was involved very early on, but that after some disagreement with the state government regarding design details such as the location of and accessibility to the airport stations, the airport authority became reluctant to participate further. From that point on, the airport was not involved in the Airport Link development, to the extent that the state and the airport took on a somewhat antagonistic attitude toward each other over the project. For instance, after the Airport Link began operating in 2000, RailCorp intended to distribute flyers advertising the Airport Link service to airline passengers arriving in Sydney at the airport, but the airport authority refused to grant permission for this activity (Wainwright 2000c). In addition, a lack of involvement from the airport prevented the kind of fare structure that might have saved the project from economic failure, such as mandatory fare inclusion in airline tickets. This would have eliminated the need for the station access surcharges that continue to inflate the ticket price of the Airport Link (and that therefore drive down ridership), but there is no way that this could have been accomplished without collaboration from the airport authority. There was also, and continues to be, no opportunity for the state government to force the airport to acquiesce to the state's policy preferences, because Sydney International Airport is under federal jurisdiction, and because since 2002 it has been owned and operated by a private company.

Finally, the managers of the Airport Link project did not undertake the kind of extensive public consultation on the project's design parameters that was conducted in Vancouver for the Canada Line. The private partner ran some limited publicity drives to local residents whom they believed might be affected by construction, and there was some effort to engage with local community groups such as the Wolli Creek Preservation Society, as mentioned in the previous chapter. However, an organized and appropriately funded program of community consultation and engagement was not undertaken for the Sydney Airport Link. Admittedly, this is typical of the Australian context, in which urban planning has a history of being conducted with minimal direct input from the public (Gleeson 2001, 146; Lahiri-Dutt 2004, 16–17); nonetheless, it is yet another facet of the state government's unwillingness or inability to engage a policy network that would have been necessary to support the development of the Airport Link.

As a result, there was effectively no network that was actively forming policy regarding a rail link from Sydney's central business district to the Sydney International Airport. There were, however, many interested actors, including the airport authority, the local municipal councils, the federal government, several private companies, the regional transit authority, the state rail transportation authority, and the general public. In other words, the potential for a collaborative governance network existed, but a lack of leadership on the part of the state government prevented the policy network from forming. Instead, the New South Wales state government attempted to handle the project alone. This may have been an effective means of service delivery in another era, but in the current period of network governance, in which multiple organizations are active in a policy area and in which partnership with the private sector is a desirable objective, failure to engage with potential collaborators can have unforeseen consequences.

Furthermore, where there were organizations with independent responsibility for transport policy in New South Wales, the state government interfered with their operations. For instance, although there was an active state-level rail authority in New South Wales, multiple interviewees commented that RailCorp was directly run by the New South Wales Department of Transport throughout the development of the Airport Link. There is no distinction made in most official documents – except, tellingly, in the final renegotiated concession agreement that was released in 2005 – between the responsibilities of the state government and those of

RailCorp in the planning and development of the Airport Link (see New South Wales 1994, for example). Government representatives made numerous comments to the press speaking as if the Airport Link were a purely government project (see Coultan 1992b for but one of copious examples). Since the beginning of the project, the media persistently referred to the state government and RailCorp interchangeably in the context of the Airport Link (e.g., Wainwright 2000d). This is in stark contrast to the Canada Line case, where the difference between government, TransLink, and CLCO was constantly stated in documents and in public statements to the media.

In the state legislature, both in the lower Legislative Assembly and in the upper Legislative Council, the Airport Link has always been discussed as if it were an exclusive project of the state government, with no attention given to input from or responsibility of RailCorp. Moreover, a reading of Hansard reveals that throughout the lifespan of the project, various government figures claimed responsibility not only for the project itself but for specific milestones (e.g., Baird 1992a, 790; Langton 1997, 9725). The government, no matter which party held power, fueled this perception that the government was in charge of the Airport Link project by regularly using the project as a partisan wedge issue. When the Liberals were in charge, the transport minister proclaimed that the Airport Link would "bring Sydney into line with many major overseas cities" but when the Labor Party had been in power "it did not attempt to provide future vision on Sydney's needs as an international city. It did nothing except run the railways into the ground" (Baird 1992a, 790). Labor, for their part, called the Airport Link "undoubtedly one of the worst decisions by a Liberal-National Government in the history of New South Wales" (Watkins 2005, 18616). Both parties frequently tried to claim credit for the Airport Link's successes and tried to blame the opposition for its failures. While this may seem like a standard feature of parliamentary government, it should be remembered that in the British Columbia legislature, the ruling Liberals continuously disavowed any responsibility for the Canada Line, calling it a TransLink project from the start (however accurate this may or may not have been).

This custom of having government politicians claim responsibility for Airport Link-related events continued even after the legal dispute occurred between the public and private P3 partners over the Airport Link's financial troubles. The restated stations agreement, which was signed after a resolution to the legal dispute was reached in 2005, specifically says that it is an agreement between RailCorp and the Airport Link Company, and goes further to state that "the Crown in the right of New South Wales is not party to any project document. RailCorp is a State Owned Corporation and does not represent the Crown. The Crown has not underwritten any agreement or guaranteed RailCorp's performance under any Project Document" (RailCorp 2005, 22). However, John Watkins, then minister of transport for New South Wales, spoke to the Legislative Assembly as if the government had renegotiated the Airport Link contract itself (Watkins 2005, 18616). Quite possibly, the government was responsible for the negotiation process but the final agreement was signed only by RailCorp. However, as previously noted, my interviews with senior officials suggest that Rail-Corp was in fact mainly directly managed by the state political executive. Further evidence of this is the fact that in 2011, the state government (and not RailCorp) announced that it would be subsidizing the station access fees at the two non-airport stations on the Airport Link's route (Saulwick 2011a).

Further displays of interference with RailCorp are highly evident. For instance, the state government restructured the rail authority several times during the years that the Airport Link was in development. Shortly before the Airport Link was announced, the state government divided the State Rail Authority's business into separate corporate divisions for passenger and freight, creating CityRail as an internal division of the State Rail Authority responsible for urban rail in and around Sydney (Moore and Lagan 1989). In 1996, after the Airport Link project was underway, the state government enacted legislation to restructure the State Rail Authority again, this time establishing an urban rail authority, CityRail (and its regional counterpart, CountryLink) as an independent corporation under the purview of State Rail and, more importantly, privatizing freight rail operations in the state (Morris 1996b). After the Airport Link had opened for service, the state government merged two formerly independent rail services companies into the Rail Infrastructure Corporation. The two former companies, which had been created earlier in the 1996 restructuring, were respectively responsible for tracks and rolling stock maintenance, and these duties were taken over completely by the new corporation (Wainwright and Connolly 2000). In 2004, the rail authority was restructured yet again: this time, the State Rail Authority and the Rail Infrastructure Corporation were reunited to create a single entity, RailCorp, now again responsible for the entire rail network, including passenger service under its CityRail and CountryLink subsidiaries (Jacobsen 2004). In 2013, CityRail was rebranded as Sydney Trains and all authority for rail transport within the state was relocated to the state department of transport. With five major restructurings in seventeen years, there was very little institutional continuity over the time period in which the story of the Sydney Airport Link was unfolding.

Continuity of personnel at the rail authority was also a problem in this time frame. Senior executives were frequently fired or transferred, often by direct intervention from the state government (see Morris 1997 for example). In the fourteen years between the announcement of the Airport Link project in 1990 and the conversion of the State Rail Authority to RailCorp in 2004, State Rail had no fewer than ten different chief executives. Several of these, like John Brew in 1995, Len Harper in 1996, and Simon Lane in 1998, were fired by the minister of transport or directly by the premier (Morris 1995a; 1997; Wainwright 2000b). This gives an average tenure of about seventeen months; by contrast, the CEO of State Rail Authority before this time period, Ross Sayers, remained in the position for four years (1988–92) before returning to work in the private sector (Coultan 1992a). By comparison, in British Columbia, TransLink had four permanent CEOs from its inception in 1999 until 2015, for an average of four years each: Ken Dobell was CEO from 1999 until he was made deputy minister to the premier in 2001, then Pat Jacobsen from 2001–08, then Tom Prendergast, who left the job when he was head-hunted to be the CEO of the largest transportation authority in North America, New York City's MTA. Prendergast was replaced by Ian Jarvis, who served as CEO until he was let go by TransLink's board of directors in 2015 during a failed bid to raise local taxes to contribute to transport funding in Vancouver.

The problem of continuity of personnel during the development of the Sydney Airport Link was true even at the political level, where not only was there an alternation of parties in power, but also the Department of Transport cycled through five ministers between 1995 and 2008, for an average of only 2.6 years each. Furthermore, more than one minister was forced out of office, including Brian Langton, who was found by the Independent Commission Against Corruption to have lied about amounts charged to his travel expense accounts (Humphries 1998). By contrast, in British Columbia, Kevin Falcon was minister of transportation for five years, from 2004–09.

Consequently, the Airport Link provided an unparalleled opportunity to exploit partisan differences. Because there was no involvement of network participants, it was phenomenally easy to characterize the Airport Link as either a government triumph or an opposition failure, no matter who was in power or when the supposed triumphs and failures occurred. There were no other actors to share the credit or the blame.

The most unfortunate consequence of this approach is that it ensured that the Labor government that inherited the Airport Link in 1995 would under no circumstances collaborate with the concessionaire beyond the absolute barest minimum requirements. The more the Airport Link experienced financial and operational trouble, the more the Labor government could effectively portray the Airport Link as a colossal failure of the previous Coalition government. According to several interview respondents, this partisan approach produced such a political advantage that the state government was led to a position where it could not be seen to cooperate with the private sector. For example, the refusal of the state government to collaborate with the Airport Link Company on marketing and advertising was described by one of my interview subjects as "not much short of open hostility." Most critically, the government refused financial support for the Airport Link Company after extremely low patronage forced it into bankruptcy, and it further refused to consider nationalizing the Airport Link outright. According to one interview subject, although this produced the best political outcome for the Labor party, it produced the worst possible outcome for the Airport Link, the partnership, the users of the service, and the taxpayers of New South Wales.

CONCLUSION

In short, the British Columbia provincial government recognized that there were numerous useful – but conflicting and competing – participants in the Canada Line's overall transportation policy network. The province succeeded in fostering a cooperative network of policy actors while positioning itself as an outside, yet ultimate, policy authority – while simultaneously managing the network through persuasion and direct manipulation. This led to a working network partnership that produced a well-developed infrastructure project with a popular design and a sound business model, as well as a P3 arrangement that consistently exhibited relatively little conflict. By supporting a functioning policy network, the province was able to attain its primary policy objective: to build a transportation megaproject on time and on budget and as an Olympic games bonus. It was mainly a balancing act – displaying active authority and achieving political objectives while at the same time nurturing cooperation within a multifaceted network of numerous autonomous participants.

In Sydney, the New South Wales state government tried to manage the Airport Link project in its entirety from the beginning, with little or no regard for the existence of, or cooperation among, network participants. There was never an attempt to foster any kind of policy network whatsoever – and yet there were multiple organizations operating within the policy sphere, several of whom (like the privately operated and federally legislated airport authority, for instance) had delegated powers of decision making that were beyond the control of the state government. Without the support of network partners, and with the discontinuity of personnel that comes with protracted political interference, the Airport Link did not experience the depth of thought, debate, and consensus that went into the design of the Canada Line. The resulting system had a flawed business plan and stakeholders who were blatantly antagonistic to each other. Subsequently, cooperation for pricing, fare collection, and marketing and advertising was not possible. Then, when conflict arose due to the bankruptcy of the private sector partner, the prominent position of the state government as the central public organization in the P3 arrangement meant that the project could be used as a partisan tool in an adversarial environment that was self-sustaining, as it yielded perceived political advantages for both parties in the legislature for many years.

6

Making Use of Policy Learning

Where do governments get ideas about the kinds of policies to pursue? Not all policies are domestic inventions. It is possible for policy goals and instruments to be transplanted from one location to another, from one time period to another, or both (Dolowitz and Marsh 1996, 344). Moreover, lessons drawn from documented experiences in other jurisdictions can be instrumental in producing desired public policy outcomes. In Sydney, decision makers did not use or were not able to use past lessons from international examples to help design the Sydney Airport Link P3, and the project resulted in governance failure. In the case of the Canada Line, knowledge about how to manage public-private partnerships – including specific techniques for interaction with the private sector, with stakeholders, and with the general public – was taken from the past experience of other jurisdictions and used to produce a stable and enduring partnership.

POLICY TRANSFER AND POLICY LEARNING:
AN OVERVIEW

There is substantial disagreement over how to categorize the various possible ways that policy can be transplanted across time and space, and numerous terms with somewhat overlapping definitions have been proposed to help identify dimensions and degrees of movement. These include: policy transfer (Dolowitz 2003), policy learning (Braun and Benninghoff 2003), policy diffusion (Simmons and Elkins 2004), policy convergence (Bennett 1991b), lesson-drawing (Rose 1991; 1993), copying (Birrell 2010), emulation (Studlar 2006), and prospective policy evaluation (Mossberger and Wolman 2003). Unfortunately, the range of related concepts is broad, and precise distinctions between these concepts are not properly described.

To complicate matters further, different authors use the same terminology to mean different things, and others use different labels for the same concepts. For example, Davies and Evans (1999) use "policy transfer" as an umbrella term meant to encapsulate many different ways through which policies can be transmitted from one location to another, while Dolowitz (2003) uses the same term, "policy transfer," to refer more specifically to the learning that takes place as one jurisdiction attempts to reproduce the successes of a policy used in another jurisdiction. Rose (1991; 1993) refers to this latter concept as "lesson-drawing," while Jenkins-Smith and Sabatier (1993) use the term "policy-oriented learning" to mean the same thing. Braun and Benninghoff (2003) simply call it "policy learning." Marsh and Sharman (2009) mainly prefer "policy diffusion" as the general term for many different mechanisms of policy movement, but they also employ "policy transfer" interchangeably with "diffusion" (although they do explain early on that they are less concerned with labels than other authors have been). Stone (2004) uses "policy diffusion" to refer specifically to the process through which similar policies can spread across multiple jurisdictions, but Studlar (2006) employs "policy convergence" and "policy diffusion" interchangeably in this context as well (but does not comment on the irony of using the words "convergence" and "diffusion" to refer to the same phenomenon). Despite attempts to unify the concepts into one grand theory (e.g., Bennett and Howlett 1992; Marsh and Sharman 2009), no convention on labelling has emerged.

The proliferation of confusing terminology notwithstanding, one thing that authors mainly agree on is that policies can be, and often are, transferred across jurisdictions, across time periods, or across both at the same time. The principal debates in this area are then mostly about how this transfer of policy can occur, how much transfer actually takes place, and what consequences are produced. While some authors refer to policy transfer as if it were occurring directly between countries (e.g., Meseguer 2005) or between institutions (e.g., Lodge 2003), many others acknowledge that there are a variety of policy actors engaged in the transfer of ideas and instruments, including politicians, bureaucrats, political parties, NGOs, the media, and corporations (e.g., Stone 1999, 55).

Therefore, before discussing how the transfer of policies from other jurisdictions operated in the cases under examination here, some terms must be defined and some concepts must be clarified. I will refer to the general concept of the use of "policies, administrative arrangements, institutions etc. in one time and/or place ... in the development of policies, administrative arrangements and institutions in another time and/or place" (Dolowitz and Marsh 1996, 344), whether through copying, emulation, learning, inspiration, coercion, or any other means, as *policy transfer*. As this suggests, there are many ways in which policy transfer can occur, such as:

1 Policy actors actively set out to learn about policies in other jurisdictions, and then either copy them or deliberately attempt to avoid their mistakes. Whether or not, and to what extent, these policy actors are able to make rational evaluations of other jurisdictions' policies is open to debate, as they will be influenced by ideologies, policy legacies and other path dependencies, institutional inertia, and biases attributable to their local political culture (Lodge 2003; Helderman et al. 2005).

2 Policy actors examine past policies from within their own jurisdiction, and learn from domestic mistakes or successes (as rationally as possible within the constraints imposed by their own local context, as above). These actors then either innovate to correct perceived errors (Rose 1993, 90–4) or reintroduce past policy.

3 Policy actors pretend that they are copying successes from other jurisdictions or other time periods (i.e., that they are learning from international examples of successes and failures), but actually they are intentionally adopting policies for ideological reasons (e.g., Lingard 2010).

4 Policy actors recommend relaxing regulation or changing tax laws in order to become more economically competitive with

other jurisdictions. This is often referred to as a "race to the bottom" (Marsh and Sharman 2009, 271).

5 Countries are pressured into adopting policies by international organizations such as the International Monetary Fund (IMF), by other countries, or by the international community (Dolowitz and Marsh 1996, 347–8).

6 Countries adopt policies through treaty arrangements with other countries, such as the North American Free Trade Agreement (Clarkson 2002).

7 Countries adopt policies because policy actors believe they need to keep up with international trends (Bennett 1991a, 43).

Undoubtedly, there are many other ways for policy transfer to occur, and this list is by no means meant to be exhaustive – it is merely intended to demonstrate that policy transfer can take on many forms.

In examining different ways that policies can be transferred, two further points arise. First, some forms of transfer are more voluntary while others are more coercive: governments that adopt and adapt policies from foreign jurisdictions in order to improve on their domestic policy outcomes are doing so of their own accord, whereas governments that make policy decisions based on directives from international money lenders like the IMF may feel that they have fewer choices available. Consequently, Dolowitz (2003) argues that modes of transfer should be viewed as a continuous spectrum, ranging from completely coercive to completely voluntary, with most forms of transfer falling somewhere in between the two extremes.

Secondly, there is an important distinction to be made between transfer that occurs for ostensibly instrumental reasons (e.g., to improve policy outcomes or to prevent perceived failures resulting from previous domestic policies) and transfer that occurs for primarily ideological reasons (such as aligning policy decisions with other jurisdictions, like reducing taxes or deregulating particular industries). No doubt, these boundaries are a bit murky, and ideologically motivated policy decisions may be presented to the public as instrumental lesson-learning. Nonetheless, policy makers can and do learn lessons about how to achieve specific policy outcomes from other jurisdictions (Rose 1991).

I will call this particular phenomenon *policy learning*, and it is probably the most studied form of policy transfer. The majority of the academic scholarship on the subject treats learning as a dependent variable – in other words, authors are mainly concerned with how learning takes place, what kinds of policies are learned, and what factors can impede or encourage the learning of policy from other time periods or jurisdictions. As public-private collaboration is still evolving, both in terms of technique and in frequency of use, it is reasonable to assume that policy actors in some countries will look to international examples of policy instruments that have been tested in other jurisdictions for guidance on the use of these instruments within their own domestic spheres. Unfortunately, the consequences of policy learning – both what learning can mean for specific policy areas and the impact of learned policies on political systems in general – is a much less studied topic.

The central debate regarding policy learning is whether or not policy can actually be learned, in the sense that there exists objective evidence that points toward successes or failures in the jurisdiction of origin that could be evaluated the same way by any observer. Some studies have taken extreme points of view: Legrand (2012) adopts the positivist epistemological position that policy learning is an instrumental activity based on objective evidence; Lingard (2010), on the other hand, presents a case from Australia in which he shows that what was reported as objective policy learning for improving standardized testing of high school students was actually an adoption of an American policy for purely ideological reasons. Most often, scholars take a less extreme approach, and it is frequently argued (e.g., Braun and Benninghoff 2003; Lodge 2003) that policies can be transferred through a process that incorporates at least some amount of rational learning as well as some influence from other forces (such as path dependencies, political culture, or specific ideological direction from the political executive). This is known as "bounded" rationality (Dolowitz and Marsh 2000), a term originally coined by Herbert Simon (1972) to express imperfect knowledge in game theoretical decision making.

In the two cases examined here, the presence or absence of bounded-rational policy learning had a discernible impact on the outcomes of particular policies. In the case of the Sydney Airport Link, decision makers did not (and to an extent, could not) actively seek lessons from other jurisdictions, and their inability to draw from potential lessons is one reason that the project resulted in governance failure. In the case of the Canada Line, efforts at policy learning – bounded-rational though they were – contributed significantly to the successful results of the partnership arrangement.

THE SYDNEY AIRPORT LINK: INADEQUATE LEARNING FROM INTERNATIONAL EXPERIENCE

In Sydney, policy learning did not take place. In part, this is due to the time frame: when the Airport Link project was first announced in 1990, P3s were not yet widely known (one interview respondent went as far as to call Nick Greiner, premier of New South Wales during the inception of the Airport Link project, the "father of PPPs" in Australia and in the world). Although some transportation infrastructure P3s had already been initiated – such as the Dulles Greenway outside of Washington, DC, which began in 1988 (Garvin and Bosso 2008, 167) – the practice had not yet achieved international popularity. Because public-private partnership was a new model at the time that the Sydney Airport Link project was first developed, neither the government nor the private sector had enough experience with partnerships to manage them successfully. It would also have been difficult (though not impossible) to locate external individuals or even organizations with substantial expertise in public-private partnerships, as there simply had not been very much time for this kind of experience to accumulate. Not surprisingly, the phrase "growing pains" was used frequently by interview respondents to refer to the beginning of the project.

These "growing pains" manifested themselves in various aspects of the project's design and planning. For instance, instead of searching for individuals with experience with P3s, the New South Wales government continued to appoint executives from within its own ranks to positions of authority over the Airport Link project. Dick Day, who was instrumental in the development of the Airport Link, had a multi-decade-long career in state rail planning that progressed through various levels of planning and management. Max Moore-Wilton, who filled a number of senior management positions in the public service at the state and federal levels and was once director general of the Department of Transport of New South Wales, was also highly influential in the Airport Link project. These people had extensive and accomplished careers as transportation planners and managers, but they did not have experience with public-private partnerships.

Similarly, the State Rail Authority did not have the opportunity to tap into a work force experienced at delivering major urban transit infrastructure. The Airport Link was the first major expansion to Sydney's urban rail network since the 1970s (Jones 2000, 7). And although the Sydney Harbour Tunnel was already under construction when the Airport Link was first announced, it was a road tunnel, not a rail project, and it therefore had a different set of requirements. State Rail did not have a readily available pool of personnel experienced with rail megaprojects, so it would have been difficult for the project's leadership to draw upon lessons from their own local experience.

As a result, the Airport Link project proceeded in a way that many of my interview subjects – who were closely involved with the project at the time – now consider to be deeply flawed. For example, research for the project was mainly conducted by local consultants or directly by the State Rail Authority (e.g., Kinhill Engineers 1994), instead of by consultants with a wider range of international experience. The result of this research was a single ridership report that dramatically overestimated patronage on the system. There is little doubt that this ridership report was inadequate: one interview subject from the private sector commented that the report was considered suspect from the beginning, and that the private partners calculated their station access fees fully expecting patronage to be lower than estimated.

Most strikingly, the Airport Link did not have a competitive tender process of any kind. Rather, as previously mentioned, the original concept was introduced to the government by the private sector unsolicited, and multiple private proponents were invited to collaborate. This is in many ways the opposite of a competitive tender process; not only were the various private competitors asked to unite their efforts, but their bids – and the eventual design of the system – were developed in collaboration with the public sector under the guidance of the state government's Department of Transport. More specifically, the original private sector partners, Transfield and CRI, signed a memorandum of understanding with the State Rail Authority to develop the Airport Link project together (Kinhill Engineers 1994). According to interviews, planning was led by a dedicated unit at State Rail, supported by a similar planning division at the New South Wales Department of Transport. According to one interviewee, there was considerable "alignment" between the public and private sector partners at this stage of the project's development.

Because of this, as has been noted, the New South Wales Independent Commission Against Corruption ordered that the development of the project be stopped in 1994, right before the concession agreement was ready to be signed. One of my interview subjects, who was familiar with the affair, told me that around the time of the ICAC investigation the New South Wales Treasury Department had advised the government to cancel the entire project, as Treasury was concerned about cost escalation directly attributable to the lack of a competitive tender process. When the private investors were informed of this, they threatened legal action, and in order to reduce the risk of substantial financial loss to the government, the mediator engaged by ICAC recommended that the project continue as planned. This narrative suggests that the private partners were able to manipulate the procurement process to their advantage – perhaps even to the extent that an official investigation into corruption in the project was cut short. Modern P3s tend to follow a more structured competitive bidding process in which collusion between bidders is actively discouraged, in order to prevent this exact outcome. When asked to comment on the unusual style used for the procurement process for the Airport Link, another interview respondent simply replied that "P3s aren't done like this anymore."

It is not surprising, then, that many interview subjects – both from the public and the private side of the Airport Link project – felt that the private partner had had too much control, especially in the early days of project development and contract negotiation. One respondent commented that the private sector consortium's "voice was too strong" and that the State Rail Authority's was too

weak. Although it may be possible to attribute this to the person-
alities of the individuals in positions of authority (as some of my
interview subjects suggested), it is equally likely that the absence of
a competitive tender allowed the private investors to gain control
over the project in a way that would not have been possible in a
more structured endeavour like the Canada Line. For example,
referring back to figure 9 in chapter 4, the Airport Link project
proceeded with the private proponents only contributing about
1.2 per cent of the total capital outlays of the project; by contrast,
the private partner in the Canada Line project contributed equity
that was worth more than 5 per cent of total project cost. One
interview respondent who is familiar with current international
practice suggested that low levels of equity like the private partner's contribution in the case of the Sydney Airport Link are often
not allowed any more, as governments increasingly demand more
money up front from private investors in order to ensure that they
maintain a long-term interest in the project.

Consequently, the most frequent comment from interviewees
was that the private proponents in the Airport Link project were
too heavily focused on the construction period, where investors
believed they would return the most quick and secure profit. The
operating period was seen as less immediately profitable, and so
it was not prioritized. One interview respondent from the private
sector provided an illustrative example of this attitude in action:
in order to minimize construction costs at the Domestic Terminal station, elevators were not extended to the departures level –
even though it could be shown that this would have attracted
more customers and would have required only a marginal increase in costs. High station access fees, which indisputably contributed to the disastrously low patronage that the Airport Link
experienced, are another symptom of this problem. Several interviewees suggested that if the private partner had been concerned
about the operating period, they may not have set the fees as high
as they did.

There are other, additional, aspects of the Sydney Airport Link
project that show an incomplete understanding of P3 governance.
For example, the state government of New South Wales did not
successfully collaborate with other governments and organizations
that would have had an interest in a rail link to Sydney Airport.

The Sydney Airport authority was not a formal (or even informal) part of the Airport Link P3; however, they have continuously shown an interest in the Airport Link, and have engaged in substantial efforts to have the station access fees reduced, including lobbying the state government and commissioning research into the effect that reducing fares would have on ridership (e.g., Booz and Co. 2010). Similarly, the federal government and the municipal councils were not involved in the project and did not contribute funding. As explained in the previous chapter, supporting policy networks has proven to be a crucial element in P3 planning and decision making.

In addition, the Airport Link project did not engage with the public or with the business community to a degree that contributed toward a successful governance arrangement. While information was shared with the public, it was mainly in reference to construction schedules and traffic disruptions. There was, according to one interview subject, a consultation event for local businesses, but it was not an ongoing institutionalized component of the project. Another interviewee described the State Rail Authority's efforts to engage local environmental groups as disorganized and "clandestine." In addition, the private sector was entirely responsible for communication with the public. One interviewee claimed to be "disappointed" that these efforts were not more evenly shared between the private and public sectors.

Lastly, and perhaps most importantly, the New South Wales state government's approach to compromise over changes to the Airport Link project is indicative of the shortage of experience that contributed to the project's failure. For example, the entire finance arrangement for the Airport Link was dictated by the private sector: according to one interview respondent with in-depth knowledge of the subject, when Transfield and CRI proved unwilling to finance the project entirely by themselves, they were asked how much capital they would be willing to provide. The figure they came up with, about $300 million, was then used by the Treasury Department to determine the private sector's ownership involvement in the project. Since it was calculated that construction of the stations would cost about that much, ownership and operation of the stations were assigned to the private sector. The state government then decided to supply the rest of the project's funding on its own. This put the state government in a position in which it would be responsible for the cost of any changes to the design of the system – which were inevitable, since the activity that was the easiest, the least expensive, and had the smallest scope had already been delegated to the private sector partner.

THE CANADA LINE:
LESSONS LEARNED AND APPLIED

In contrast to the Airport Link case, policy transfer in general and policy learning in particular are integral components of the story of the development of the Canada Line. From the beginning, the aim was to learn about international P3 experiences on which the Canada Line project could be based. To this end, the Canada Line's project managers commissioned numerous consultant reports on a wide variety of topics, including ridership forecasting, alignment, economic feasibility, and environmental considerations. Many of these reports were prepared by consulting companies with an international presence, such as Halcrow, IBI Group, KPMG, PricewaterhouseCoopers, and Booz Allen Hamilton (e.g., IBI Group 2001; Halcrow Group Limited 2003; PricewaterhouseCoopers 2003). By 2001, these consultants had likely accumulated considerable international experience on public-private partnerships, and would have been able to employ this experience in the preparation of advice for the Canada Line's decision makers.

Furthermore, public sector employees working on the Canada Line project conducted direct investigation of past experience in other jurisdictions. For example, it was acknowledged early on that tunnel excavation would very likely disrupt business activity along the length of the route. Business liaison committees, in an effort to mitigate the impact of construction, were charged with maintaining communication with local businesses, as well as providing support through improved signage and advertising so that the public would be aware that businesses were still in operation during the construction period. According to interview respondents, this model was based on practices that had been used successfully in Toronto, Boston, and Los Angeles during recent infrastructure expansion in those cities. This also indicates that the Canada Line's decision makers searched for lessons from beyond the narrow limits of airport rail projects.

Substantial professional experience was accessed through the hiring of individuals who had worked on public-private partnerships in other jurisdictions at the executive level. Pat Jacobsen, CEO of TransLink from 2001 to 2008, had previously been deputy minister of transportation in Ontario, where she helped develop the $3 billion Highway 407 P3 for the Ontario government. Jeff Hewitt, senior vice president of engineering for the Canada Line, had been a senior engineer on the massive Taiwan High Speed Rail P3. Ron Aitken, who was a project manager for TransLink during the Canada Line project, had previously been director of project management for Bombardier, a Canadian company that at that time already had considerable experience in international P3 endeavours. In this way, significant accumulated experience with international practice in public-private partnerships was available at the highest levels of decision making.

Relatedly, the Canada Line project had access to considerable professional experience on public transit infrastructure megaprojects that had been built in British Columbia. Jane Bird, who was CEO of Canada Line Rapid Transit Inc., had been an executive on the previous extension to Vancouver's urban rail system, the Millennium Line. Dan Doyle, whose thirty-six-year career with the British Columbia Ministry of Transportation started in an engineering position and ended as deputy minister, later sat on the board of directors of CLCO as well as Partnerships BC, and was an instrumental figure in the 2007 restructuring of TransLink. Larry Ward, who held several executive positions at TransLink before becoming chief operating officer of Protrans BC (the private operator of the Canada Line), had also been involved with the Millennium Line at the executive level. And John Eastman, who was senior vice president technical for Canada Line Rapid Transit, had been the lead project manager for the Millennium Line and before that a senior engineer on the first arm of Vancouver's SkyTrain system, the Expo Line.[1]

---

1 This information was revealed by interview subjects, but not necessarily by the individuals named here.

As a result of this accumulated experience, the Canada Line was an exceptionally well-organized and informed project. A vast amount of research was done by consultants, by Canada Line project management, and by the cities of Vancouver and Richmond. This included multiple ridership forecasts, based on data on traffic patterns in the Vancouver region (e.g., Halcrow Group Limited 2003), financial feasibility studies (PricewaterhouseCoopers 2003), station design and placement reports (Spaxman Consulting Group 2003), and extensive public consultation efforts (e.g., Kirk and Co. 2003). All of this research was conducted before the private sector partner was brought on board, and most of it before the tender process even began (see RAV Project Management Ltd. 2003). The project was so thoroughly prepared for the private sector that the request for proposals included a draft contract, on which the final concession agreement was based (compare RAV Project Management Ltd. 2004a with RAV Project Management Ltd. 2005a, for example).

In other words, knowledge about international P3 examples allowed decision makers responsible for the Canada Line to run a sophisticated development process. For example, the Canada Line's private sector procurement was conducted as a multi-stage, multi-year tender. At each stage, some competitors were eliminated and continuing candidates were invited to strengthen their proposals. The process was competitive, and collusion between the private sector bidders was not allowed (although each of the bidders was a consortium composed of several separate companies). A retired Canadian judge, Ted Hughes, was engaged to ensure that the procurement process was conducted fairly (see RAV Project Management Ltd. 2004b, for example). This represents a highly evolved P3 development process, especially in comparison to an earlier P3 procurement like the Sydney Airport Link, which did not abide by a rigid structure and did not have multiple competitive stages.

During the Canada Line's development, considerable effort was taken to include as many stakeholder parties as possible. Notably, this included the cities of Vancouver and Richmond, who were given more or less equal status with the federal government and the Vancouver Airport Authority, as previously mentioned. Many of my interview subjects, representing various organizations, commented that the cities were considered full partners and that there was no appreciable hierarchy among any of the stakeholder parties. Interviewees reported especially favourably on the level of engagement that the Canada Line had with the City of Vancouver, and several confirmed that even after the contract with the private partner was signed, cooperation with the city governments was crucial to the success of the project. This refers to small details, such as the city's quick provision of permits for construction purposes and road closures, as well as more serious cooperation, such as the relocation of the Broadway-City Hall station or the redesign of the southern tunnel portal, both of which the City of Vancouver requested and the project's management implemented. This positive relationship with multiple partners and stakeholders ensured support from a wide group of institutional participants and, like the tender process, is indicative of an advanced understanding of the prerequisites for a successful P3 project.

The Canada Line's project managers also interacted greatly with the public, which benefitted the project in several ways: it allowed for very reliable ridership forecasting; it provided political legitimacy for the project (see Synovate 2004 for example); and it likely helped contain backlash from business owners whose businesses were disrupted by construction efforts. Although there was major legal action on this matter from businesses in the Cambie Village area, the plaintiffs represented a minority of the businesses that were affected by the construction, and they were concentrated along only one section of the construction route. And, according to one interview subject, the Cambie Village Business Association originated with the Canada Line's Business Liaison program – in which case the efforts in public consultation for the Canada Line permanently increased cohesion and strengthened social capital among the local business community.

Finally, when the private partner in Vancouver was unable to meet the project's funding requirements, the project itself was altered. Stations were removed from the design, a connector to the cruise ship terminal was cancelled, and the Richmond terminus was built as a single track instead of a double track, among other things (Canada Line Rapid Transit Inc. 2006). Interview respondents commented on how some aspects of the project were reallocated to TransLink's operating budget, such as the bicycle path under the Canada Line's Fraser River crossing.

In other words, the approach to the private sector's involvement for the Canada Line was very different than that of the Airport Link. In Vancouver, when faced with lower-than-expected private finance, the project scope was reduced to meet the financial requirements. In Sydney, the same issue was addressed by increasing the scope and thereby increasing the government's financial contribution. This is exemplified by the re-addition of the Wolli Creek interchange station, which was negotiated out of the Airport Link project because of the way the private partner's capital contribution was allocated, but which was then added back into the project at full cost to the state government. From one perspective, the apparent eagerness of the government of New South Wales to get the Airport Link project done at any cost may have given the private partner a disincentive to negotiate or compromise, whereas the pragmatic and patient approach adopted in Vancouver – as learned by observing the past experiences of other P3 projects – resulted in a stable and successful partnership arrangement.

It should be noted that the Canada Line project was not, as is to be expected in a modern democratic state, a completely rational enterprise based on instrumental decision making. In addition to active evaluation of lessons from international experience, the concept of a P3 finance and operation structure for the Canada Line was copied from other jurisdictions in Canada and elsewhere when the provincial Liberal Party came to power in 2001. Before that time, partnership with the private sector had not been formally adopted for the Canada Line. In fact, in the twenty years after a rapid rail transit line connecting Vancouver and Richmond was first mentioned in the debates of the provincial legislature of British Columbia in 1973, private finance was not seriously considered. This includes the time period after active planning for the project began in 1990 under the Social Credit government of Bill Vander Zalm (Johnston 1990, 11026).

In 1993, New Democrat minister of finance (and later premier) Glen Clark announced that private finance and operation – in other words, public-private partnership – was being considered for this transit project (Clark 1993, 7889). However, the government at the time had its reservations about using a P3 for urban transit, citing concerns that partnership would not reduce the debt burden on the province and that it could require onerous government guarantees to the private sector in order to be feasible (Clark 1995, 1595o). Research on the potential for a P3 finance and operating structure for the project was continued by the newly established transit authority in 2000 (RAV Project Management Ltd. 2003), and a consultant report in 2001 listed the "exploration of possible private sector partnerships and financing strategies" as one of the principal goals of the project (IBI Group 2001), but no final decisions were made. In addition, the P3 model had a significant opposition, especially at the municipal and metropolitan levels (e.g., Bula 2003b). So although the P3 format had been proposed and investigated, it was not sufficiently accepted by policy makers prior to 2001 to ensure at that point that it would be used for the project.

In 2001, the Liberal Party was elected to office in British Columbia, and from the beginning of their mandate they made market liberalization a priority in many sectors. This included deregulation, the downsizing of government operations, increased engagement with the private sector, and public-private partnerships, all of which was especially targeted at the transportation sector (Perl and Newman 2012). It is not surprising, then, that despite the controversy surrounding the use of P3 for the Canada Line, and in spite of the uncertainty maintained by previous governments about the benefits of partnership with the private sector for this project, the provincial Liberal government in 2002 clearly mandated that the Canada Line would proceed as a P3 or it would not proceed at all.

The British Columbia Liberals did not, however, invent the public-private partnership. As the Sydney case confirms, P3s for the development of transportation infrastructure had been attempted outside of British Columbia prior to 2002. In fact, many other jurisdictions, including European countries, US states, and other Canadian provinces, had already experimented with P3 infrastructure development with mixed results (e.g., Bradford 2003; Garvin and Bosso 2008; Koppenjan and Enserink 2009). Moreover, the provincial Liberal government directly mentioned the use of P3s in other jurisdictions as a model for their use in British Columbia, in Throne Speeches (e.g., British Columbia 2002, 10), and they collaborated with other Canadian provinces on the development of P3s in the transportation sector (Western Transportation Ministers Council 2005). But P3s as an instrument for infrastructure development had not garnered much enthusiasm until the Liberals were elected to power. The use of P3s for transportation infrastructure had been, at best, under skeptical consideration for many years – until the provincial Liberal government took steps to import P3 ideas from other jurisdictions.

Therefore, while the use of P3s in British Columbia is certainly an example of policy transfer, it would be much more difficult to show that there was any kind of learning involved at this level. This is because the attention given to P3s by the Liberal provincial government, including the establishment of Partnerships BC and the requirement of P3 for the Canada Line, was the result of actions that came directly from the political executive. There is no public debate or evidence of deliberation that would be required to show that alternatives were considered and rejected. In other words, although it is likely that politicians in British Columbia knew of the use of P3s for transportation infrastructure in other parts of the world and based their decisions on these international examples, there is insufficient evidence to confirm that formal evaluative efforts were conducted. More likely, this is an example of the ideological transfer of policy ideas without learning.

Learning did occur later, however, as evidenced by the flurry of consultant reports and direct investigations that were conducted in an attempt to establish best international practice for the project after the decision to use the P3 format was made. This is what Dolowitz and Marsh (2000) and others mean by policy learning through "bounded rationality": the provincial government mandated a P3 structure for the project, and once this was accepted, policy makers were free to learn from international examples within the constraints imposed by the P3 model. Given these constraints, a purely rational exploration of all policy options for the Canada Line was not possible; instead, choices for policy direction were limited to those that had shown positive results in other time periods and in other locations *within the P3 format.*

CONCLUSION

In his analysis of the banking sector in the UK, Hall (1993, 278) defines policy learning as "a deliberate attempt to adjust the goals or techniques of policy in response to past experience and new information." Hall's analysis was directed at state-level paradigm changes – such as the market-oriented paradigm brought forward by the Liberal party in British Columbia following their election in 2001 – rather than at specific policy instruments like public-private partnerships. However, the principle is the same. As Dolowitz and Marsh (2000, 12) have noted, programs for the implementation of specific policies can be transferred in the same manner as broader policy paradigms. In the case of the Canada Line, there was a deliberate attempt to adjust the techniques used to implement the project, including many aspects of the P3 arrangement, in response to past international experience. In the case of the Sydney Airport Link, similar attempts at learning from international experience were not undertaken, in part because of the much smaller body of experience that was available at the time that the Airport Link was developed. Put plainly, there was less international evidence on successful strategies for P3s available to policy makers responsible for the Sydney Airport Link than there was for decision makers involved in the Canada Line. The Airport Link's planners would have had to work harder to make the most of whatever evidence was available. This kind of situation, in which new policy problems emerge on an international scale, can create serious obstacles to learning from lesson-drawing (Rose 1993, 83).

One corollary of this last statement is that the Canada Line had access to an international body of experience precisely because early attempts at transportation P3s like the Sydney Airport Link encountered difficulty. As lessons about successful and unsuccessful strategies for P3s accumulated over time, there would have been a larger bank of ideas for the Canada Line's decision makers to draw on than was available to policy makers in the case of the Airport Link. In other words, the success of the Canada Line may have been contingent on the failure of other similar projects in other jurisdictions, upon which policy makers in Vancouver were able to draw lessons. This suggests that as policy lessons accrue over time, jurisdictions with similar norms and ideological frames of reference will converge on similar policy options. In fact, this phenomenon (called policy diffusion or policy convergence by some authors) has been observed previously (Stone 2004; Studlar 2006). From this perspective, the problems that the Airport Link and other projects from the same time period experienced were necessary steps in the global evolution of transportation P3s.

As explained earlier, the reintroduction of public-private partnerships, in transportation as well as in other sectors, represents a fundamental shift in the way that public services are delivered and therefore how the state is democratically directed. The shift to governance is a structural change to the way that the state allocates scarce resources. It seems improbable that such a change could happen without friction. Policy learning can therefore be seen as a requirement for success in P3s because the adoption of P3s and other collaborative policy instruments cannot be expected to fall into alignment with previous modes of public service delivery without producing some degree of conflict.

In Sydney, the state of New South Wales attempted to introduce P3s into the transportation sector without the benefit and employment of knowledge of previous examples of similar policy instruments. The result was a poorly designed governance arrangement that produced a chain of events leading to governance failure and subsequent long-term consequences for state-level politics. First, a lack of competition for the private component of the P3 led to a powerful private partner that was able to influence the terms of the arrangement. Then, a lack of foresight into the financial model of the partnership allowed the project to proceed with a very low equity contribution from the private sector, which led to a prioritization of more immediate avenues for profit – such as favouring the construction period over the operating period. This focus on quick profit motivated the private sector to set the station access fees so high as to deter customers. Inadequate research on the demand for the service produced a faulty ridership forecast, which, combined with the high fees, meant that the Airport Link would be severely underused for more than a decade. This led to financial difficulty for the private sector partner, which led to legal action against the state, which resulted in financial loss to the state government and ultimately to the people of New South Wales. In contrast to this, policy makers responsible for the Canada Line project made extensive use of bounded-rational policy learning to produce a sophisticated P3 arrangement that safeguarded the project against many of the pitfalls that were experienced by the Airport Link.

In addition to learning from previous examples of P3 arrangements in other jurisdictions, policy makers involved with the Canada Line produced a substantial domestic innovation in P3 implementation – the use of an independent, collaboratively structured project management corporation to direct the design and procurement phases of the project. This will be the subject of the next chapter.

7

Innovation:
Collaborative Project Management

In the last chapter, I explained how policy makers responsible for the Canada Line were able to prevent governance failure in part by learning from an international body of experience in decision making for P3s. Sometimes, however, policy problems do not have a record of established solutions, either internationally or domestically. In these cases, policy makers must innovate their own solutions and thereby become trendsetters (Rose 2004, 108).

The Canada Line project was faced with a problem that is increasingly common in the era of governance: there were multiple organizations, from both the public and private sectors, who were either interested in, or partly responsible for, policy areas that were affected by the project. Ten years prior to the Canada Line, policy makers responsible for the Sydney Airport Link attempted to solve this same problem by ignoring stakeholders and network participants and imposing traditional government hierarchy on the various actors involved in the project. As a result, the state government of New South Wales took primary responsibility for the Airport Link project, and centralized decision making and interaction with the private sector participants through the state's Department of Transport. While central government authority may have been a conventional strategy in the days when welfare state programming and government intervention were on the rise, the trend in the current era is toward devolution, decentralization, and inter-organizational governance – which means that command and control government strategies are no longer as appropriate for policy formulation and implementation. In Vancouver, policy makers adopted a different approach to this problem, and created an independent project management company, CLCO, to oversee the entire project from concept to operation. This company was established as an independent, separately incorporated subsidiary of TransLink, and its creation helped the Canada Line avoid the governance problems that afflicted the Sydney Airport Link.

INSTITUTIONALIZING COOPERATION

The primary purpose of having CLCO manage the Canada Line (rather than TransLink directly) was to institutionalize cooperation among the multiple public and private sector organizations that were involved with the project. CLCO, as has been mentioned, was wholly owned by TransLink. However, TransLink did not have full operational control over this subsidiary. CLCO's board of directors was made up of representatives from all four of the project's funding partners (TransLink, the provincial government, the federal government, and the Vancouver Airport Authority). Because these organizations were forced to collaborate on decision making for CLCO, their cooperation over the Canada Line was ensured as a fundamental component of the structure of the project, with no party able to take full control.

Several interview respondents commented on the ability of CLCO to resolve conflict between the various partners. Because all contact – among the public sector partners, between the public sector and the airport, and between all parties and the private sector proponent – was conducted through CLCO, there was very little potential for friction to arise. All communication had to be done through an independent body that was jointly controlled by all parties. One interview subject commented that there had been some tension between the private partner and TransLink, due to mutual suspicion over the terms of the P3 agreement, as well as some general dissatisfaction from TransLink over the fact that it was not in control of the project. However, this same interviewee claimed that CLCO was instrumental in eliminating this friction, because it ensured that TransLink and the private sector had very little contact. Also, the multipartite nature of CLCO meant that although TransLink was not totally in control, neither was any other single entity – it was a combined effort. This assuaged feelings of discontent at TransLink.

In other words, part of CLCO's function was to broker the divergent interests of all the parties involved in the Canada Line project. This not only refers to the official partners as mentioned above, but also includes unofficial partners, such as the City of Vancouver, the City of Richmond, the business community, and the general public. As discussed in previous chapters, CLCO engaged heavily with the public in consultation over the design of the system, and created a highly effective business liaison program that was mostly well received by the business community, especially in the downtown core of Vancouver and in Richmond. Moreover, the existence of CLCO allowed the City of Vancouver, which was not an official funding party and therefore had no authority over the project, to have access to the private sector proponent at the executive level.

Furthermore, because the board of CLCO was composed of directors representing multiple organizations, the company was required to be responsible to a variety of sometimes diverging interests. This is a slightly different function than ensuring cooperation and minimizing conflict. In addition to being an interest broker and a peacemaker, CLCO was also compelled to appease numerous masters individually – organizations that could have differing political requirements. In order to ensure that the needs of all of its stakeholders were met, CLCO proceeded with an abundance of caution, frequently surpassing its minimum legal obligations on many policy decisions in a variety of areas. If CLCO had been responsible to only one government or organization, this may not have been necessary.

For example, CLCO decided early on that it would combine the federal and provincial environmental assessment procedures, and ensure that the project was compliant with the more stringent of the two. In fact, the provincial environmental requirements were stricter, and they were also not legally required because the line was shorter than the twenty kilometres necessary to invoke the provincial assessment process (federal environmental assessment would have been required regardless, since the route crossed a federal waterway and terminated on federal land at the airport).

Nevertheless, CLCO elected to go beyond its minimum legal requirements and harmonize the two environmental applications (RAV Project Management Ltd. 2003, 65). In another example, CLCO requested that the provincial auditor general review the Canada Line's competitive procurement process "as an added accountability measure that is consistent with best emerging practice" (RAV Project Management Ltd. 2005e, 3). This was in addition to the review of the procurement process that had been conducted by the Canada Line's "Fairness Auditor," retired judge Ted Hughes (see Hughes 2003 for example).

Of course, CLCO was only in existence during the design and construction phases of the Canada Line project. Once the system went into operation in 2009, CLCO was disbanded and responsibility for liaison with the private sector reverted to TransLink. However, the P3 arrangement governing the operation and maintenance of the Canada Line is intended to last for thirty years of operation. It is not difficult to believe that the culture of collaboration, and especially of cautious decision making, that was established and fostered by CLCO will last into the operating phase.

In fact, after the Line went into operation and CLCO was dissolved, TransLink continued the practice of proceeding cautiously on policy decisions. In October 2009, TransLink applied to the regional Transportation Commission[1] to approve its proposed surcharge on Canada Line trips to the airport. Previously that year, the Transportation Commissioner had ruled that this was not necessary – that TransLink could levy a surcharge on airport trips without applying to the Commission for approval (TransLink Commission 2009). Nevertheless, TransLink pushed forward with its application for review, which in the end was only partially approved, and then subsequently amended, by the Commission (monthly pass holders were exempted from the proposal).

Although CLCO's board of directors was composed of representatives from the various public sector funding organizations, one of the central conditions of the CLCO board was that no elected officials should sit as a director. Many of the directors were inde-

1 The TransLink Commission was an independent provincial office that had oversight responsibilities for public transit decisions. It was dissolved in 2014.

pendent representatives chosen as technical experts (such as Eva Matsuzaki, a prominent Vancouver architect who had worked on the iconic Provincial Courthouse building in downtown Vancouver) or as experienced members of the business community (like Larry Bell, who served on numerous corporate boards and was CLCO's chairman). One of my interview subjects, who was familiar with the CLCO board, commented that they were not completely certain that all of the provincial and federal government nominees on CLCO's board were regularly reporting to their representative governments. This meant that although CLCO was responsible to several different public sector organizations, including three levels of government (federal, provincial, and regional metropolitan, through TransLink), it was functionally independent of direct political involvement, especially including partisan considerations.

CLCO was therefore placed in a unique position where it was required to be sensitive to the political needs of its partner organizations but was not subject to direct political interference. One outcome of this position was the heightened aversion to risk in decision making described above. In addition, because none of its board members were elected politicians, CLCO was protected from lobbying and from the pressures of the electoral cycle. One interview subject reported that a convention arose where CLCO would not hold public media events of any kind with politicians during an election campaign at any level of government. This resulted in "a build-up of milestone events during elections" according to this interviewee, because the self-imposed convention meant that they could not hold press conferences or media events to promote the milestones.

And lastly, the use of CLCO as a procedural focal point for the Canada Line project meant that all public relations for the project emanated from a single source. The high level of continuity of personnel assured that the same central messages were broadcast throughout the development of the project. Repeated communications included the idea that the project was "on time and on budget" and the fact that the Richmond-Vancouver corridor is home to "one-third of the region's jobs and 20% of its population" (see RAV Project Management Ltd. 2004c for example). Statements such as these were ubiquitous in press releases and public statements published by CLCO, and were repeated by the private media (e.g., Bellett 2007b). This frequent and regular repetition of claims about the Canada Line – without conflicting messages from multiple organizations – helped to concretize public opinion about the project.

The CLCO model, then, is one of an independent, ostensibly politically neutral, and publicly owned project management firm. The collaborative, representative nature of CLCO's board ensured that the interests of its various stakeholders were met, while conflict was kept under control and political interference minimized. In response to pressure from having to meet the requirements of all stakeholders simultaneously, CLCO exhibited highly careful decision making and resisted the influences of political partisanship as much as was possible. Decision making was portrayed at all times as united, and public relations were consistent throughout.

CLCO'S POLITICAL FUNCTION

Although CLCO may have deflected political interference while conducting its project management duties for the Canada Line, the company was fundamentally as much a political vehicle as it was an administrative device. In addition to the instrumental and institutional functions of CLCO described above, its creation and operation fulfilled a number of political objectives as well.

An illustrative example of CLCO's political role relates to the official name of the organization. Upon creation, it was known as Richmond-Airport-Vancouver Project Management Ltd., as the project was originally referred to as the Richmond-Airport-Vancouver Rapid Transit Project or RAV Line, both in official documents and in the provincial legislature. From 2002 until 2006 the company was frequently referred to as RAVCO, short for Richmond-Airport-Vancouver Company. However, as has been previously noted, the federal government insisted that the project be renamed the "Canada Line" as part of the agreement to secure federal funding for the project. In 2006 the company officially changed its name to Canada Line Rapid Transit, Inc. to reflect this change, and has been referred to as CLRT or CLCO in various sources since. My interview subjects most frequently referred to the company as CLCO, and since most of these individuals were familiar with the project either at the administrative or the political level, that is the abbreviation that I have adopted here.

The name change from RAVCO to CLCO is significant because it served to lend official support to the notion that the Canada Line was not a project of the provincial government of British Columbia. The provincial government had been using the RAV acronym on all documents and in all publicity until the funding agreement with the federal government was signed. Calling the project the "Canada" Line allowed them to give an official name to their stance that the project was not under their control (see Falcon 2007, 6461 for example). In fact, the naming of the project and of the project management company quickly took on a partisan flavour, since after 2006 the opposition in the legislature and other outspoken critics referred to the project as "RAV Line" and the company mainly as RAVCO, while the government and all parties attached to the project referred to the project as "Canada Line" and the company as CLCO. For several years it was possible to identify the Canada Line's supporters and detractors simply by which name they chose to use to describe the project.

This impression of the provincial government as a detached funding agency yielded significant political benefits. First and foremost, it granted the provincial government immunity from the divisive debates that were held at the municipal and regional levels over the financing of the line. While the province clearly favoured a P3 financing structure for the project, the illusion that the final decision was in the hands of the metropolitan government allowed the province to avoid any backlash from opponents of P3s (when the proposal was approved) or supporters of P3s (if the Line had been rejected). This is equally true for the technology of the Line (street-level light rail versus automated and grade-separated rapid rail) and its alignment (tunnelling under Cambie Street as opposed to using an existing, but more remote, right-of-way along Arbutus Street), both of which incited a vigorous and bifurcated public debate, as has been previously discussed. Because the municipal councils, through the regional metropolitan government, felt that they had the authority to approve or reject the project, the province was spared from the animosity that developed as the issue generated considerable polarization (see Bridge 2003 for example).

Likewise, having CLCO take complete control over the administration and management of the project meant that the province could not be blamed for any discontent caused by the development of the project itself. This applies to accusations of impropriety in the procurement process (since the British Columbia public sector pension fund was one of the private investors of the Canada Line; see Gentner 2006, 3935), but would also include decisions about the route, the location of stations, and the design of the stations or trains, which in any project of significant public interest are bound to appeal to some and provoke dissatisfaction in others.

Most materially, allowing CLCO to present itself as the project management authority of the Line meant that the province was indemnified from responsibility over the inevitable disturbance caused to residents and businesses by the system's construction. As has been mentioned, most of the Canada Line's presence in the city of Vancouver was constructed using the "cut and cover" method of tunnel excavation, which causes noise, appreciable levels of dust, increased truck traffic on residential routes, reduced availability of parking, road closures, and reduced pedestrian access. One section of the route required blasting with dynamite (RAV Project Management Ltd. 2005d). Construction-related disturbances to residents, and especially to businesses, are what motivated the lawsuits pursued against the Canada Line that were discussed in chapter 4.

Consequently, the use of CLCO as the organization responsible for the Canada Line largely protected the provincial government from liability against these lawsuits. In the first case, the "Do RAV Right Coalition," a group of business owners in the Cambie Village area of the Canada Line's construction route, sued the project assessment director of the provincial Environmental Assessment Office, claiming that he had erroneously granted an environmental assessment certificate to CLCO to allow it to begin construction on the Canada Line. That staff member at the Environmental Assessment Office was the only representative of the province named in the suit, and CLCO was implicated as a respondent responsible for the Canada Line. No other parties were identified.

In a second lawsuit, the owner of a maternity clothing store on Cambie Street sued CLCO, the City of Vancouver, TransLink, the province of British Columbia, the Canada Line's private sector partner, and the government of Canada. In this suit, the business owner contended that the change of construction method from deep-bore tunnelling to cut and cover caused a significant disturbance to her business and that she should be awarded financial compensation. Although the case progressed through two appeals to the Supreme Court of Canada, it was dismissed at that level and decided in favour of the Canada Line. In the original judge's decision, all claims against the provincial government were dismissed because CLCO *was actually the legal owner of the Canada Line* and the province could not be shown to have been an active partner in the project beyond its financial contribution (*Heyes v. City of Vancouver 2009 BCSC 651*: para. 168).

Another benefit of having CLCO act as the principal agent in charge of the Canada Line is that it shielded the project from the automatic auditing responsibilities of the provincial auditor general. Since CLCO was incorporated as a subsidiary of TransLink, it was effectively a private corporation at arm's length from the government, and was not subject to the automatic auditing that applies to normal government activity (Strelioff 2004). In fact, while the project has been proclaimed many times to have been "on time and on budget" (e.g., Yaffe 2010), a formal audit has never been released to the public.

These last two points raise some important questions about the degree of accountability that was evident in the Canada Line project. As discussed in chapters 1 and 3, one of the theoretical advantages of public-private partnerships is that they are supposed to bring accountability to private enterprise through the contractual involvement of the government. In a perfectly free market, where producers have full knowledge of the needs of their customers and consumers have complete information on the products they are buying, competition might generate superior customer service that could act as a proxy for accountability (Rufín and Rivera-Santos 2012, 1638). In other words, in such a market, customers can use their dollars to vote, and market winners could therefore be the most transparent, the most environmentally friendly, the least corrupt, and so on. In infrastructure, no such market exists, as was examined in chapter 2. Large transportation systems are natural monopolies in which single operators provide services for lengthy contract periods, with competition occurring only in isolated bursts at the procurement stage and later at the contract renewal stage. In theory, then, government involvement is required to ensure accountability and transparency.

The way that CLCO shielded the government from negative feedback implies that this accountability function of the government was somehow impaired in the case of the Canada Line. However, in any P3, accountability is nearly always circumscribed (Shaoul et al. 2012). In a P3, contracts and negotiations with private proponents are usually confidential documents, so as to prevent competitors from tampering with the bidding process. Furthermore, accountability and transparency are provided by supervision from the government, not by direct observation; citizens will need to trust their government representatives to provide information on the activities of the private partner, because this information will not be openly available (the current ridership numbers for the Sydney Airport Link are not available to the public, for instance, because they are considered a trade secret necessary to ensure the competitiveness of the Airport Link Company). Therefore even in the best of circumstances, the government partner in a P3 can only provide a layer of accountability on top of a necessarily private business venture.

This is precisely how accountability operated with respect to the Canada Line. The provincial government of British Columbia was in fact the paramount authority with responsibility for the Canada Line, despite its desire to appear otherwise. First, as chapter 5 argued, Canadian provinces have complete constitutional supremacy over city governments, including the regional government of Metro Vancouver. Second, the province has statutory power over TransLink, as the transportation authority was in fact created by provincial statute. And regardless, total legal superiority of the province over CLCO, TransLink, and Canada Line is written into the Provincial Funding Agreement (British Columbia 2005, 36–7) and the concession agreement with the private partner (RAV Project Management Ltd. 2005a, 42).

Furthermore, the provincial government asserted its authority over the Canada Line on several occasions, often creating momentous turning points in the project's development. The provincial government declared its funding contribution to be contingent on the project's being financed as a P3; by doing so, even though it was clear from public statements that municipal politicians were against P3 financing, the province established what would end up being the most important aspect of the structure of the project. This decision, and the provincial funding proposal that followed it, also effectively rearranged the transportation priorities list for TransLink and for the Metropolitan government. If the province had not put its foot down on the P3 issue, but had instead offered unconditional funding and let TransLink set its own priorities, Vancouver would have had a non-P3 extension to its northeastern suburbs instead of a Canada Line to Richmond and the airport; the northeast extension was the next project on the regional transportation plan, and the majority of local politicians were against P3 financing.

There were several other occasions in which the province's interference in the Canada Line project also proved to be highly influential. After the metropolitan politicians voted against the Canada Line in 2004, the provincial government persuaded them to reconsider their decision, first by cancelling the parking stall tax that was supposed to fund public transit service enhancements (Bula 2004a) and then by threatening to take over the Canada Line project in its entirety (Read et al. 2004). One of my interview subjects commented that this last proposal was not taken advantage of because the province had indicated that it would only take care of procurement and construction, but that the operation of the system would still be left to TransLink. However, the fact that the province was willing and able to make such an offer indicates its level of confidence in its legislative superiority over the transportation authority and over local governments. If not for the provincial government's active participation and leadership, the Canada Line would likely never have happened.

In the end, the province of British Columbia successfully pursued a strategy of positioning itself as a hands-off funding entity while presenting CLCO as functionally in charge of the Canada Line. This strategy had the effect of directing any discontent surrounding the project at CLCO and not at the government. In this way, political penalties were not paid by the governing party. Then, after the Canada Line went into operation, CLCO was dissolved, and any public dissatisfaction with the Canada Line disappeared with it. Any lasting praise that the Canada Line garnered – either in its construction phase or later in its operating phase – now accrues directly to the provincial government because CLCO is no more. CLCO deflected blame away from the government while it existed, but then when the project turned out to be a budget and patronage success, CLCO was gone and the provincial government could take the credit. Likewise, if the project had been a bust, the government could easily have blamed TransLink, which was after all the legal owner of CLCO.

Nevertheless, the province had never relinquished its supreme statutory authority over the project and its policy area, so accountability – as much as is available in a P3 arrangement – was ultimately preserved. If there had been any devastatingly serious backlash against the project, or if corruption had been uncovered in any of the public or private sector participants, the government could have exercised its authority and intervened. But since this was not required in the case of the Canada Line, the provincial government used mostly indirect means to enforce its most controversial decisions and was therefore able to escape public discourse on the topic.

PROJECT MANAGEMENT STYLES COMPARED

There were two main factors that formed the nucleus of the Sydney Airport Link's later problems: first, the ridership estimate was wrong by a wide margin. A system that was built for 65,000 riders per day only received 10,000 per day in its first five years of service. Second, and relatedly, the price was too high. At 400 per cent of the price of a similar ride on the rest of the transit network, the station access fees actively deterred commuters from using the Airport Link. These two factors hampered the urban development goals of the project, created a system that was simply not used to its full expected potential, and enabled a political conflict in the state legislature that compelled the party in power to reject compromise and refuse to collaborate with the private sector on a solution.

Unlike the Canada Line, the Airport Link did not have a central collaborative organization. The design and development of the system was undertaken by the private sector, with input from Rail-Corp and the state's Department of Transport. The state government did hire a project management group to oversee the government's interest in the construction phase of the project (see Kinhill Engineers 1994), but they were hired for a limited time period to perform specific tasks, and were brought in late in the project's development cycle. In Vancouver, by contrast, CLCO was a foundational decision-making body, essential to the project and placed in a role of primary leadership.

As a result, a frequent comment from my Australian interview respondents was that the Airport Link project had considerable alignment of interests during the development phase, but not nearly enough for the operating phase. The focus of the construction phase of the project was to ensure that the project opened on time and did not surpass its budget by a significant amount. There was less concern with the operating parameters of the line, which had lasting implications (like the very high station access fees, for example). Also, because collaboration had not been institutionalized in Sydney as it later was in Vancouver, it was very easy for the government to cease to collaborate with the private sector as soon as the operating phase began and low ridership became evident.

If the state government of New South Wales had used a management approach similar to the model used for the Canada Line, the governance failure that occurred in Sydney would not have happened. For one thing, a more cautious project management company would have produced a better patronage forecast, either by better specifying the design parameters, by commissioning more than one study, or by relying on independent consultants. This is what CLCO did in the case of the Canada Line, and their ridership predictions were much more accurate (in fact, as has been shown, the ridership forecast for the Canada Line *under*estimated patronage).

Secondly, a better ridership forecast would have allowed for a different price point for the station access fees, or a different funding model altogether. A more accurate prediction of how many people would actually use the system, combined with an economic analysis of the elasticity of demand of the product, would have yielded a more realistic surcharge from which the private sector could gain a return on its investment. The more modest surcharge applied for the Canada Line, along with a repayment scheme that does not allow the private operator to set fares, produced a more financially sustainable system in that case. Because there was no independent central organization in charge of collaboration for the Sydney Airport Link, the fee structure was entirely ignored by the state government, as it was seen as being the responsibility of the private sector partner. More central, collaborative planning on this front would have saved the project from financial disaster.

Additionally, once the Airport Link went into service and its shortcomings became immediately apparent, if there had not been so much to be gained politically from disavowing the project, the New South Wales Labor government could have implemented any of several options to mitigate disaster and ensure that the project would achieve its public service objectives. These options included supplying temporary financial relief to the private sector partner; renegotiating the concession to change the fee structure; establishing better cooperation over marketing and advertising; negotiating a partnership with the airport authority; or purchasing the system outright. If a CLCO-like institution or a similar approach had been used in Sydney, it is probable that some kind of relief plan would have been implemented, in part because there would not have been the same kind of political motivation to abandon the project but also because the institutionalization of cooperation would have allowed for a more collaborative solution to the governance failure that occurred.

In the absence of a central CLCO-like institution in the Sydney case, the state government was exposed to all of the public's dissatisfaction with the Sydney Airport Link. The central position of the state government meant that all of the political consequences attached to public perception of the Airport Link project accrued directly to the state. For example, the Liberal government under John Fahey had positioned the Airport Link prominently as a major public infrastructure investment project in their 1995 election campaign, which they lost (Wainwright 2000e). A poll in 2002 showed that the Australian public was still very skeptical of P3s (Morris 2002); in 2003, shortly after a state election, the minister of transport specifically referred to the airport rail link "disaster" as a reason for not using a P3 to extend the rail system to the western suburb of Paramatta (Kerr and O'Malley 2003). Labor premier Kristina Keneally's move in 2011 to use public funds to subsidize fares at two Airport Link stations was referred to as "a last-minute pork barrel" (Saulwick 2011a), as it came one month before a state election, and all four airport stations were in the former premier's riding of Heffron. Throughout its history, the Airport Link has been a high-profile political issue, and one with which state governments have always been closely associated.

Similarly, the Sydney Airport Link did not benefit from the negotiated compromises that CLCO facilitated in Vancouver. Because the public sector side of the Airport Link project was controlled directly by the state government, policy decisions were a function of the will of only one government entity – the political executive. This means that "caution" in decision making was subject only to the strategy that was perceived as being best suited to the government's political ambitions – there was no need to be sensitive to the requirements of multiple organizations. In addition, the direct contact between elected politicians and the management of the Airport Link meant that it was fairly easy for the government to use the project as a partisan wedge issue – even before patronage levels became a problem (e.g., Langton 1997, 9724). This would have been much more difficult in Vancouver, where the non-partisan nature of CLCO acted as a barrier to this kind of direct politicization of the Canada Line project.

CONCLUSION

In Vancouver, CLCO was a key factor in the prevention of governance failure. CLCO created the cohesion that connected the public sector partners, kept stakeholders informed, enabled careful oversight of policy decisions, and maintained a functioning relationship with the private sector. CLCO allowed the provincial government to retain control of the Canada Line without appearing to dictate the policy direction of the project, which had the effect of quelling dissenting opinions, reducing potential conflicts, and generally fostering an atmosphere of collaboration. In Sydney, the central control of the project by the state government had the opposite effect, making conflict not only possible, but inevitable.

8

Conclusion

It should be evident by now that governance arrangements can most certainly fail. In public-private partnerships in the transportation sector, as exemplified by the Sydney Airport Link, governance failures can prevent a governance arrangement from producing the outputs it intended to, such as having a useful rail route that commuters actually use, minimizing traffic congestion, promoting urban development, reducing greenhouse gas emissions, or other stated policy objectives. In the Sydney case, a governance failure appeared as a cessation of cooperation between the public and private partners as a result of the dramatic financial collapse that occurred shortly after the service went into operation in 2000. In the case of the Canada Line in Vancouver, all of the governance arrangement's policy objectives were met, and collaboration between the partners continues without significant issue.

The consequence of governance failure for the people of New South Wales is that they did not receive a viable rail link between Sydney's central business district and Sydney International Airport. While the Link is there, and the trains are running, it is not used to its fullest capacity because of the high ticket price. Therefore the policy objectives of the project have not been fulfilled. In addition, substantial public funds have been diverted to the project as a direct result of the governance failure, including money that was lost when the P3 contract was renegotiated. If governance failure had not occurred in this case, this money could have been used in other areas of public policy.

But why did governance failure occur in the Sydney case? The easy (but ultimately unsatisfying) answer is that the Sydney Airport Link was not a case of governance failure at all, but a case of financial failure, which occurred because of a faulty patronage forecast and an unrealistic pricing model. By this reasoning, if a better ridership forecast had been provided, the project would have been priced differently, or designed differently, and it would have achieved financial success and therefore it would also have achieved its public policy objectives.

This is, however, not a satisfactory explanation, for two reasons. One, the above does not explain how a faulty ridership forecast was allowed to occur in the first place; and two, it does not explain why, when faced with crisis, the P3 partners in the Airport Link project were not able to reconcile their differences and work toward a solution. If there had been no governance crisis, then a swift resolution would have been expected, rather than a five-year legal battle ending in a renegotiated contract and ongoing subsidies that represent a significant loss of funds to the public purse.

On the contrary, as I have shown, the Airport Link project experienced a failure in governance and not just a failure of finances. The state government of New South Wales categorically refused to collaborate with the private sector to resolve the financial conflict brought on by the underestimation of patronage. The Labor government of the day seized on the opportunity to label the Airport Link as a fiasco of the previous Liberal government, and was subsequently determined to see the Airport Link Company go bankrupt. This was (perhaps correctly) considered to be the best way to make a political statement that the Liberal government had negotiated a bad deal over the Airport Link. This strategy required the government to stand back and allow the bank to foreclose on the Airport Link Company's debt, because the worse the outcome for the Airport Link Company, the more compelling the government's argument would be that their Liberal predecessors had set the project up for failure.

In fact, the Airport Link continued to be politically relevant long after the financial crisis was resolved and a new private partner had been brought on board, indicating that the Labor Party's strategy was perceived (by them, at least) to be productive. In 2005, when announcing the restructuring of the P3 agreement, then minister of transport and deputy premier John Watkins gave an impassioned speech in the legislature detailing this "bungled project" that his predecessors – voted out of office ten years prior – had initiated when they were in government (Watkins 2005, 18616). As late as 2011, six years after the P3 contract was renegotiated and eleven years after the Airport Link went into service, then premier Kristina Keneally told the Sydney Morning Herald that "the expensive fees on the Airport Link were a legacy of the previous Liberal government, which signed off on the public-private partnership" (Saulwick 2011a). This strategy of blame assignment also absolutely prohibited the Labor government from nationalizing the Airport Link (and thereby officially and legally accepting ownership of the project), although this might have been the most cost-effective way to end the conflict and emerge with a rail system that meets its stated public policy objectives. All of these were tactics pursued by an extremely successful Labor Party government, which was in power in New South Wales for sixteen years.

But more fundamentally, a faulty patronage forecast and an unrealistic ticket price were allowed precisely because there was insufficient policy leadership emanating from the state government at every point along the project's trajectory. If the government had consulted a broader policy network of interested actors, it would have been able to produce more than one ridership report, and it would have been able to acquire data that would have better illuminated the estimation process. It would also have been able to produce a better overall business model, such as one that included the airport's authority to charge fares directly through airline tickets, which would have eliminated the need for station access fees altogether. If the state government had had access to more international experience on P3 best practices, it could have insisted on a rigorous competitive tender process, which would have produced a better designed system, a better business model, and more accurate ridership estimates. If a collaborative project management entity had been employed, the entire project would have been developed with more careful decision making. This would have produced a better pricing mechanism, a cooperative relationship between the public and private sector partners that could have become institutionalized, and a government that – shielded from political backlash – would not have found it as easy and as necessary to engage in a high-stakes partisan campaign resulting in the bankruptcy of the system. These are all things that were employed in the Vancouver case, where governance failure did not happen (and does not appear likely to happen in the future, either).

According to another explanation, the difference in outcomes between these two cases is due to the fact that a turnover in government occurred in New South Wales during the Airport Link episode, while the Liberal party was in power in British Columbia for the entire development of the Canada Line. This explanation must be rejected, for two reasons: firstly, serious planning for the Canada Line, including the beginning of an organized effort between multiple public sector agencies, began in 1999 when the New Democrats were still in power; and secondly, the Liberals did not make any effort (though they had ample opportunity) to use a transit megaproject for partisan purposes when the Canada Line's predecessor, the Millennium Line, failed to reach its ridership estimates for years after opening (Luba 2005).

Another alternative explanation is that the governance arrangement did not fail in Sydney, but that the state government simply unilaterally refused to collaborate. Under this explanation, if the government had offered support, the financial collapse would not have happened and perhaps a settlement could have been reached that would have enabled the project to realize its public service goals.

Again, this explanation is not satisfactory. The state government of New South Wales engaged in behaviour that could be seen as uncooperative because the weaknesses of the governance arrangement for the Airport Link project compelled it to do so. Because the government was directly responsible for the project, they were required by the nature of the party system to attempt to assign the blame for the project's collapse on the opposition party. If they had nationalized the system or if they had settled the crisis in any way that employed direct financial assistance to the Airport Link Company, they would have been seen as accepting blame for the failure of the project and spending more public money to resolve it. In the end this is what happened, but because the public subsidies are small and are delivered by means of ongoing installments, they are perceived as being less politically damaging than a large lump-sum payment would have been. Because the Airport Link's business model was designed to have the private sector carry the patronage risk in its entirety (as user fees were its only source of revenue), the Labor government was forced to allow the Airport Link company to go bankrupt, in order to show how big a mistake this Liberal-designed business model was. From a public service delivery perspective, this may not have been the best approach; but from a partisan perspective, this strategy could easily have been perceived to yield the biggest gains.

More generally, the issues of governance failure that were encountered in the case of the Sydney Airport Link underscore a broader debate on the role of the state in the delivery of public services. For more than half of the twentieth century, many advanced democracies made considerable efforts to develop a system which is often referred to as the welfare state. In this system, many benefits were conferred on citizens in a mainly universal (as opposed to residual) manner and funded in theory (though not always in practice) by mechanisms of progressive taxation. The benefits of the welfare state, now often tellingly referred to as entitlements, raised standards of living, stimulated and stabilized economies, reduced class conflict, and institutionalized public service delivery as a means of democratically allocating scarce resources to subsets of a population.

Since the early 1970s, a public attitude developed in which citizens increasingly saw the public sector as wasteful, rent-seeking, unresponsive, and tied up in pointless bureaucratic process. Political parties in many countries were elected to office on platforms that included marketization of services and New Public Management reforms of the public sector, as well as reducing government activity and lowering taxes. Since 1980, many of these promises have been fulfilled, and governments have sold state-owned enterprises, reduced regulation of industry, contracted operations to the private sector, downsized the public service, and generally increased market activity in many areas.

However, possibly because of an attachment to the entitlements of the welfare state era, citizens have not demanded (nor have governments produced) a return to the pre-welfare state level of service delivery. Instead, governments, autonomous public agencies, private not-for-profit entities, independent authorities, and private corporations all operate together to deliver public services in an increasingly decentralized and non-hierarchical arena. This system

of governance, in which public-private collaboration is a prominent method of service delivery, is still evolving, and the appropriate role of the state within the system is still a contested issue.

Governance, as opposed to the traditional methods of *government*, is now an essential method of public service delivery in
many countries and in many sectors. As such, governance has
become a key element of democracy itself. Public-private partnerships, which are formal contractual arrangements between the
public and private sectors, are a popular form of governance often
seen as effective (they achieve objectives of public service delivery)
and efficient (they achieve their objectives at minimum cost).
These public-private partnerships are used especially in sectors
where large capital investments are required and where user fees
can easily be charged or, at the very least, calculated so that payments per user can be effected.

However, like markets and governments acting alone, governance arrangements – including P3s – can fail. When they fail, governance arrangements can cause collaboration between the public
and private sectors to break down, leading to a situation in which
the objectives of the partnership cannot be achieved.

Cases of governance failure can help address the broader issues
of the role of the state in governance. Public-private partnership is
usually presented as a way for the private sector to bring efficiency
and discipline to infrastructure delivery. Fundamentally, the logic
of P3s and other methods of alternative service delivery is to
remove the state from the implementation side of the service delivery equation; the state – which proponents of P3s characterize as
bloated, slow, wasteful, and prone to delay – should be relegated to
broad policy direction while the efficient and innovative private
sector should be charged with the actual delivery of services to the
public. In the face of some P3s that did not realize these goals of
increased efficiency or that failed to meet their public service
objectives, some observers have argued that even more private sector involvement – not less – is required for P3s to be effective
(Mustafa 1999; Poschmann 2003; United Nations 2008, 37–8).

However, in order to prevent governance failure from occurring, the state must provide sufficient policy leadership. In other
words, it is not sufficient for the government to retreat into the
realm of policy ideas; the state must have an active and authori-

tative engagement with the delivery of public services. In the case of P3s for the development of transportation infrastructure in particular, the examples of the Sydney Airport Link and Vancouver's Canada Line suggest that a government that is actively engaged in the management of its governance arrangement with the private sector can prevent governance failure, while a government that bestows too much responsibility on the private partner and ignores network participants leaves the partnership vulnerable to failure.

Specifically, I have shown three ways in which leadership from the government can help prevent governance failures from occurring. First, governments must pay attention to policy networks. P3s are networks of public and private sector actors, but they are also nested within more general networks of public sector agencies, stakeholder organizations, business groups, and private companies. By paying attention to the needs of the relevant policy networks, and by fostering cohesion and cooperation, governments can contribute to a collaborative environment in which as many interested parties as possible are included in the decision-making process. At the same time, the government must position itself as a clearly defined but distant authority, visibly ready to step in and correct governance failures as soon as they appear. In short, the government must manage the policy network to achieve the best balance between independence and interconnectedness of the network's actors. In Vancouver, the provincial government of British Columbia achieved this balance through careful manipulation of network actors, and through active engagement with as many relevant potential network participants as possible. In Sydney, the New South Wales government completely ignored the possibility of a policy network and attempted to act independently. In an era of governance, where jurisdictions and responsibility for policy are shared with numerous public and private sector actors, this approach is simply not viable.

Second, governments must learn from past experiences in other jurisdictions. They must establish what has worked, and what has not, as seen through the bounded-rationality lens of the domestic political context. Lessons from other jurisdictions in other time periods can prove to be highly educational, especially for governments that have not undertaken similar projects on their own in the past. In Vancouver, policy learning was critical to the success experienced by the Canada Line. In Sydney, policy learning did not take place – but admittedly, this is mostly due to the fact that the Sydney Airport Link was developed at a time when P3s for transportation infrastructure were relatively new, so there was not yet an international body of experience available to draw upon for policy examples. This suggests that there is a natural evolution to global knowledge and understanding of new policy problems, as some authors have proposed (Rose 1993; Stone 2004).

And third, policy makers in Vancouver innovated a new method for project management that provided a central focus to the project and to the governance arrangement. This collaborative institutional model for project implementation enabled the government to protect itself from any public discontent over the project while, at the same time, it allowed the government to retain ownership of the success of the project in the long term. In addition, the use of CLCO institutionalized cooperation among the P3 partners and fostered a sensitivity to the needs of the multiple funding organizations in a way that inspired the project to proceed with extreme caution in decision making. In Sydney, the use of a CLCO-style organization would have obviated the need for partisan conflict by placing an institutional barrier between the government and the partnership; it would also have provided a more institutionalized collaborative arrangement with the private sector that would have been more difficult to abandon at the first appearance of crisis.

This study has, of course, some limitations. First, it should be noted that this project only considered two case studies. In order to achieve a more robust generalization, more cases should be studied. As the global inventory of public private partnerships grows, in transportation and other areas, further study will be more easily accomplished.

However, the two cases analyzed here do provide some convincing results. In Vancouver, a careful government expertly guided the governance arrangement for the Canada Line according to international lessons and an innovative project management approach, and thereby avoided governance failure. In Sydney, two inexperienced governments of different political stripes set up a public-private partnership with some inherent weaknesses that left it particularly susceptible to a governance failure. Because the two cases are so similar in terms of technical design, political motivation, and cultural and legal contexts, but so different in terms of policy implementation, it is evident that the steps taken by policy makers in the case of the Canada Line helped to prevent governance failure while the absence of these strategies likely contributed to governance failure in the case of the Sydney Airport Link. If the public sector in Sydney had been more able or more willing to supply strategic policy leadership, then the Airport Link would not have experienced governance failure.

References

Abdel Aziz, Ahmed M. 2007. "Successful Delivery of Public-Private Partnerships for Infrastructure Development." *Journal of Construction Engineering and Management* 133 (12): 918–31.

Adam, Silke and Hanspeter Kriesi. 2007. "The Network Approach." In
Theories of the Policy Process, edited by Paul A. Sabatier, 129–54. Boulder, CO: Westview Press.

Aikins, Stephen K. 2009. "Political Economy of Government Intervention in the Free Market System." *Administrative Theory and Praxis* 31
(3): 403–8.

Alberta Transportation. 2012. "Construction Digs-in on Final Leg of
Edmonton Ring Road: Final Leg of Anthony Henday Drive Set to
Open to Traffic in 2016." Alberta Government News Release, 16 July.
Edmonton: Government of Alberta.

Albinski, Henry S. 1973. *Canadian and Australian Politics in Comparative
Perspective*. New York: Oxford University Press.

Allan, John R. 2001. *Public-Private Partnerships: A Review of Literature and
Practice*. Regina: Saskatchewan Institute of Public Policy.

Almqvist, Roland and Olle Högberg. 2005. "Public-Private Partnerships
in Social Services: The Example of the City of Stockholm." In *The
Challenge of Public-Private Partnerships*, edited by Graeme Hodge and
Carsten Greve, 231–56. Cheltenham, UK and Northampton, MA:
Edward Elgar.

Ansell, Chris and Alison Gash. 2008. "Collaborative Governance in Theory and Practice." *Journal of Public Administration Research and Theory*
18 (4): 543–71.

Arnouts, Rikke and Bas Arts. 2009. "Environmental Governance Failure:

The 'Dark Side' of an Essentially Optimistic Concept." In *The Disori-*
ented State: Shifts in Governmentality, Territoriality and Governance,
edited by Bas Arts, Arnoud Lagendijk, and Henk Van Houtum,
201–28. Wageningen and Nijmegen, Netherlands: Springer.

Asenova, Darinka and Matthias Beck. 2003. "A Financial Perspective on
Risk Management in Public-Private Partnership." In *Public-Private*
Partnerships: Managing Risks and Opportunities, edited by Akintola
Akintoye, Matthias Beck, and Cliff Hardcastle, 127–51. Oxford, UK:
Blackwell.

Atkinson, Michael M. and William D. Coleman. 1992. "Policy Networks,
Policy Communities and the Problems of Governance." *Governance* 5
(2): 154–80.

Aucoin, Peter. 1995. *The New Public Management: Canada in Comparative*
Perspective. Montreal: Institute for Research on Public Policy.

Baird, Bruce. 1991. "Light-Rail Claims Are Premature." *Sydney Morning*
Herald, 9 May, 9.

– 1992a. "Sydney (Kingsford-Smith) Airport-City Rail Link." *Full Day*
Hansard Transcript (Legislative Assembly), 6 March, Corrected Copy.

– 1992b. "Sydney (Kingsford-Smith) Airport Third Runway." *Full Day*
Hansard Transcript (Legislative Assembly), 28 October, Corrected Copy.

Ball, Robert. 2011. "Provision of Public Service Infrastructure – The Use
of PPPs in the UK and Australia: A Comparative Study." *International*
Journal of Public Sector Management 24 (1): 5–22.

Barry, Michael P. 2014. "The Loss of Crimea: How Much Does Ukraine
Lose, and How Much Does Russia Gain, a Computable General Equilibrium Model." *Journal of Global Peace and Conflict* 2 (1): 103–19.

Batley, Richard. 2001. "Public-Private Partnerships for Urban Services." In
The Challenge of Urban Government: Policies and Practices, edited by
Mila Freire and Richard Stren, 199–214. Washington, DC: World Bank
Institute.

Bator, Francis M. 1958. "The Anatomy of Market Failure." *The Quarterly*
Journal of Economics 72 (3): 351–79.

Bauch, Hubert. 2010. "Is Too Much Talk Toxic?" *The Gazette* (Montreal),
6 November 2010, B3.

Bellett, Gerry. 2007a. "Things Not So Bad Along Cambie Construction
Zone, Business Board Member Says." *The Vancouver Sun*, 5 May 2007.
B2.

– 2007b. "Canada Line 'On Time, On Budget." *The Vancouver Sun* 6 September 2007, B1.

Bennett, Colin J. 1991a. "How States Utilize Foreign Evidence." *Journal of Public Policy* 11 (1): 31–54.

– 1991b. "What Is Policy Convergence and What Causes It?" *British Journal of Political Science* 21 (2): 215–33.

Bennett, Colin J. and Michael Howlett. 1992. "The Lessons of Learning: Reconciling Theories of Policy Learning and Policy Change." *Policy Sciences* 25 (3): 275–94.

Birkland, Thomas and Sarah Waterman. 2008. "Is Federalism the Reason for Policy Failure in Hurricane Katrina?" *Publius: The Journal of Federalism* 38 (4): 692–714.

Birrell, Derek. 2010. "Public Sector Reform in Northern Ireland: Policy Copying or a Distinctive Model of Public Sector Modernization?" *Public Money and Management* 30 (2): 109–16.

Boardman, Anthony E., Finn Poschmann, and Aidan R. Vining. 2005. "North American Infrastructure P3s: Examples and Lessons Learned." In *The Challenge of Public-Private Partnerships*, edited by Graeme Hodge and Carsten Greve, 162–89. Cheltenham, UK and Northampton, MA: Edward Elgar.

Boei, William. 2004. "RAV Line Sent Back to the Drawing Board: TransLink Kills Project, Looks for Cheaper Option." *The Vancouver Sun* 8 May 2004, A1.

– 2005. "RAV Ditches Tunnel Plans for Two Major Streets." *The Vancouver Sun* 27 January 2005, A1.

Bond, Shirley. 2009. "Estimates: Ministry of Transportation and Infrastructure." *Official Report of Debates of the Legislative Assembly (Hansard)*, 7 October 2009. Afternoon Sitting, Volume 4, Number 3.

Booz and Co. 2010. *Impact of Fare Reform on the Sydney Airport Rail Link.* Final Report to Sydney Airport Corporation Limited, February 2010.

Borins, Sandford F. with Lee Brown. 1986. *Investments in Failure: Five Government Enterprises that Cost the Canadian Taxpayer Billions.* Toronto: Methuen.

Bovens, Mark, Paul 't Hart, and B. Guy Peters. 2001. "Analysing Governance Success and Failure in Six European States." In *Success and Failure in Public Governance: A Comparative Analysis*, edited by Mark Bovens, Paul 't Hart, and B. Guy Peters, 12–29. Cheltenham, UK and Northampton, MA: Edward Elgar.

Bradford, Neil. 2003. "Public-Private Partnership? Shifting Paradigms of Economic Governance in Ontario." *Canadian Journal of Political Science* 36 (5): 1005–33.

Braid, Kyle. 2004. "GVRD Residents On Rapid Transit." Ipsos-Reid Press Release No. 2279, 16 June.

Braun, Dietmar and Martin Benninghoff. 2003. "Policy Learning in Swiss Research Policy – The Case of the National Centres of Competence in Research." *Research Policy* 32 (10): 1849–63.

Bridge, Maurice. 2003. "RAV Prompts Questions of Private-Public Pacts." *The Vancouver Sun* 28 May, D4.

British Columbia. 2002. "Speech from the Throne." *The Opening of the Third Session, Thirty-Seventh Parliament of the Province of British Columbia*, 12 February.

– 2005. "Provincial Funding Agreement (Restated) among Greater Vancouver Transportation Authority and Province of British Columbia (as represented by the Minister of Transportation) and RAV Project Management Ltd. concerning the Richmond • Airport • Vancouver Rapid Transit Project." Provincial Funding Agreement effective 5 November 2004 (final release 29 March 2005).

– 2007. *Shareholder's Letter of Expectations Between the Minister of Finance (as Representative of the Shareholder, the Government of British Columbia) and the Chair of the Partnerships British Columbia (as Representative of the Corporation)*. Signed 25 April by Partnerships BC and 1 May by the Government of British Columbia.

British Columbia Ministry of Transportation and Infrastructure. 2009. "Canada Line by the Numbers." *Information Bulletin No. 2009TRAN 0002-000047*, 14 January. Victoria: British Columbia Ministry of Transportation.

British Columbia Ministry of Transportation and Infrastructure and TransLink. 2010. "Canada Line Celebrates First Year of Service." *News Release No. 2010TRAN0053-000956*, 17 August, Victoria: British Columbia Ministry of Transportation.

Brock, Kathy L. 2005. "Delicate Dances: New Moves and Old Steps." In *Delicate Dances: Public Policy and the Nonprofit Sector*, edited by Kathy L. Brock, 1–15. Montreal and Kingston: McGill-Queen's University Press.

Brody, Howard. 2010. "Medicine's Ethical Responsibility for Health Care Reform – The Top Five List." *The New England Journal of Medicine* 362 (4): 283–5.

Bryson, John M., Barbara C. Crosby, and Melissa Middleton Stone. 2006. "The Design and Implementation of Cross-Sector Collaborations:

Propositions from the Literature." *Public Administration Review* 66 (Supplement S1): 44–55.

Buchanan, James M. 1975. *The Limits of Liberty: Between Anarchy and Leviathan*. Chicago: University of Chicago Press.

Bula, Frances. 2003a. "Council Approves RAV Line." *The Vancouver Sun*, 16 May, A4.

– 2003b. "RAV Line Gets the Green Light After a Tight GVRD Vote." *The Vancouver Sun*, 29 May, A1.

– 2004a. "2 TransLink directors Set Conditions for Voting Yes on RAV." *The Vancouver Sun*, 15 May, A1.

– 2004b. "New RAV Deal Would Cap Price." *The Vancouver Sun*, 25 June, A1.

Bula, Frances and Jim Beatty. 2004. "Province Okays Extra $65m as RAV Line Heads to Final Vote." *The Vancouver Sun*, 1 December, A1.

Bult-Spiering, Mirjam and Geert Dewulf. 2006. *Strategic Issues in Public-Private Partnerships: An International Perspective*. Oxford: Blackwell.

Burgess, David F. and Glenn P. Jenkins, eds. 2010. *Discount Rates for the Evaluation of Public Private Partnerships*. Kingston and Montreal: McGill-Queen's University Press.

Burns, Peter and James G. Gimpel. 2000. "Economic Insecurity, Prejudicial Stereotypes, and Public Opinion on Immigration Policy." *Political Science Quarterly* 115 (2): 201–25.

Campbell, Gordon. 2004. "Estimates: Office of the Premier." *Official Report of Debates of the Legislative Assembly (Hansard)*, 20 May 2004. Afternoon Sitting, Volume 25, Number 19.

Campbell, Murray. 2006. "407 Tolls Won't Be Rolled Back." *The Globe and Mail*, 1 April, A15.

Canada Line. 2006. "Contract Confirms Public Protected From Potential Construction Cost Increases: Concession and Funding Agreements Available on Project Website." *Canada Line Information Bulletin No. 14*, 3 March.

Canada Line Rapid Transit Inc. 2006. *Canada Line Final Project Report: Competitive Selection Phase*. 12 April. Vancouver: Canada Line Rapid Transit Inc.

Cardew, Richard. 2003. "Privatisation of Infrastructure in Sydney, Australia." In *Infrastructure Provision and the Negotiating Process*, edited by Frank Ennis, 117–34. Aldershot, UK: Ashgate.

Cervin, Naomi. 2000. "Private Prisons: Should Crime Pay?" *Auckland University Law Review* 9 (1): 48–77.

Clark, Glen. 1993. "Estimates: Ministry of Finance and Corporate Relations." *Official Report of Debates of the Legislative Assembly (Hansard)*, 25 June 1993. Morning Sitting, Volume 11, Number 16.

− 1995. "Estimates: Ministry of Employment and Investment." *Official Report of Debates of the Legislative Assembly (Hansard)*, 21 June 1995. Afternoon Sitting (Part 2), Volume 21, Number 10.

Clarkson, Stephen. 2002. *Uncle Sam and US: Globalization, Neoconservatism, and the Canadian State*. Toronto: University of Toronto Press.

Coghill, Ken and Dennis Woodward. 2005. "Political Issues of Public-Private Partnerships." In *The Challenge of Public-Private Partnerships*, edited by Graeme Hodge and Carsten Greve, 81–94. Cheltenham, UK and Northampton, MA: Edward Elgar.

Cohn, Daniel. 2008. "The New Public Autonomy? Public–Private Partnerships in a Multi-Level, Multi-Accountable, Political Environment: The Case of British Columbia, Canada." *Policy and Society* 27 (1): 29–42.

Coleman, William D. and Anthony Perl. 1999. "Internationalized Policy Environments and Policy Network Analysis." *Political Studies* 47 (4): 691–709.

Compston, Hugh. 2009. *Policy Networks and Policy Change*. Basingstoke, UK and New York: Palgrave Macmillan.

Corden, Max. 2003. *40 Million Aussies? The Immigration Debate Revisited*. Melbourne: Productivity Commission.

Cornerstone Planning. 2003. "Step 1: Individual/Group Consultation: Interim Summary Report." *Report on Phase 2 of the RAV Project Pre-Design Public Consultation*. Cornerstone Planning Group, 15 December.

Coulson, Andrew. 2008. "Value For Money in PFI Proposals: A Commentary on the UK Treasury Guidelines for Public Sector Comparators." *Public Administration* 86 (2): 483–98.

Coultan, Mark. 1992a. "State Rail Chief to Quit This Year." *Sydney Morning Herald*, 25 May, 2.

− 1992b. "Airport Train Needs Land To Be Developed." *Sydney Morning Herald*, 29 October, 5.

− 1994. "Govt in Push for Airport Tunnel." *Sydney Morning Herald*, 3 January, 1.

Cruz, Carlos Oliveira and Rui Cunha Marques. 2013. "Flexible Contracts to Cope with Uncertainty in Public–Private Partnerships." *International Journal of Project Management* 31 (3): 473–83.

Cummins, Carolyn. 2006. "Green Square Facelift Continues." *Sydney Morning Herald*, 16 September, 58.

Daniels, Ronald J. and Michael J. Trebilcock. 2000. "An Organizational Analysis of the Public-Private Partnership in the Provision of Public Infrastructure." In *Public-Private Policy Partnerships*, edited by Pauline Vaillancourt Rosenau, 93–109. Cambridge, MA: MIT Press.

Davies, Jonathan and Mark Evans. 1999. "Understanding Policy Transfer: A Multi-Level, Multi-Disciplinary Perspective." *Public Administration* 77 (2): 361–85.

de Bettignies, Jean-Etienne and Thomas W. Ross. 2004. "The Economics of Public-Private Partnerships." *Canadian Public Policy* 30 (2): 135–54.

Demetri, George. 2007. "Canada Line is on Track to Cut Vancouver Congestion." *Tunnelling and Trenchless Construction*, May.

Derthick, Martha and Paul J. Quirk. 1985. *The Politics of Deregulation.* Washington, DC: The Brookings Institution.

Dewulf, Geert, Anneloes Blanken, and Mirjam Bult-Spiering. 2012. *Strategic Issues in Public-Private Partnerships, 2nd ed.* Chichester, UK: Wiley.

Dixon, John and Rhys Dogan. 2002. "Hierarchies, Networks and Markets: Responses to Societal Governance Failure." *Administrative Theory and Praxis* 24 (1): 175–96.

Dixon, Timothy, Gaye Pottinger, and Alan Jordan. 2005. "Lessons from the Private Finance Initiative in the UK." *Journal of Property Investment and Finance* 23 (5): 412–23.

Dollery, Brian, Joel Byrnes, and Lin Crase. 2008. "Structural Reform in Australian Local Government." *Australian Journal of Political Science* 43 (2): 333–9.

Dolowitz, David P. 2003. "A Policy-maker's Guide to Policy Transfer." *Political Quarterly* 74 (1): 101–8.

Dolowitz, David and David Marsh. 1996. "Who Learns What from Whom: A Review of the Policy Transfer Literature." *Political Studies* 44 (2): 343–51.

– 2000. "Learning from Abroad: The Role of Policy Transfer in Contemporary Policy-Making." *Governance* 13 (1): 5–24.

Drucker, Peter F. 1974. *Management: Tasks, Responsibilities, Practices.* New York: Harper & Row.

Dunn, James A. Jr. 2000. "Transportation: Policy-Level Partnerships and

Project-Based Partnerships." In *Public-Private Policy Partnerships*, edited by Pauline Vaillancourt Rosenau, 77–91. Cambridge, MA: MIT Press.

Engel, Eduardo, Ronald Fischer, and Alexander Galetovic. 2013. "The Basic Public Finance of Public–Private Partnerships." *Journal of the European Economic Association* 11 (1): 83–111.

Esping-Andersen, Gøsta. 1999. *Social Foundations of Postindustrial Economies*. Oxford: Oxford University Press.

Falch, Morten and Anders Henten. 2010. "Public Private Partnerships as a Tool for Stimulating Investments in Broadband." *Telecommunications Policy* 34 (9): 496–504.

Falcon, Kevin. 2005. "Estimates: Ministry of Transportation." *Official Report of Debates of the Legislative Assembly (Hansard)*, 26 October. Afternoon Sitting, Volume 3, Number 7.

– 2007. "Estimates: Ministry of Transportation." *Official Report of Debates of the Legislative Assembly (Hansard)*, 27 March. Morning Sitting, Volume 17, Number 3.

Faulkner, Keith. 2004. "Public-Private Partnerships." In *Public-Private Partnerships: Policy and Experience*, edited by Abby Ghobadian, David Gallear, Nicholas O'Regan, and Howard Viney, 65–70. Basingstoke, UK and New York: Palgrave Macmillan.

Flinders, Matthew. 2005. "The Politics of Public–Private Partnerships." *British Journal of Politics and International Relations* 7 (2): 215–39.

Flyvbjerg, Bent, Nils Bruzelius, and Werner Rothengatter. 2003. *Megaprojects and Risk: An Anatomy of Ambition*. Cambridge, UK: Cambridge University Press.

Friedman, Milton. 1962. *Capitalism and Freedom*. Chicago: University of Chicago Press.

Galambos, Louis and William Baumol. 2000. "Conclusion: Schumpeter Revisited." In *The Rise and Fall of State-Owned Enterprise in the Western World*, edited by Pier Angelo Toninelli, 303–9. Cambridge, UK: Cambridge University Press.

Garvin, Michael J. and Doran Bosso. 2008. "Assessing the Effectiveness of Infrastructure Public Private Partnership Programs and Projects." *Public Works Management Policy* 13 (2): 162–78.

Gentner, Guy. 2006. "Estimates: Ministry of Energy, Mines and Petroleum Resources." *Official Report of Debates of the Legislative Assembly (Hansard)*, 24 April 2006. Afternoon Sitting, Volume 9, Number 7.

Gerhager, Barbara and Anwer Sahooly. 2009. "Reforming the Urban

Water Supply and Sanitation (UWSS) Sector in Yemen." *Water Resources Development* 25 (1): 29–46.

Gillen, David W. and William Morrison. 2004. "Airport Pricing, Financing and Policy: Report to National Transportation Act Review Committee." In *The Economic Regulation of Airports: Recent Developments in Australasia, North America and Europe*, edited by Peter Forsyth, David W. Gillen, Andreas Knorr, Otto G. Mayer, Hans-Martin Niemeier, and David Starkie, 45–62. Aldershot, UK; Burlington, VT: Ashgate.

Gleeson, Brendan. 2001. "Devolution and State Planning Systems in Australia." *International Planning Studies* 6 (2): 133–52.

Goodwin, Mark. 1998. "The Governance of Rural Areas: Some Emerging Research Issues and Agendas." *Journal of Rural Studies* 14 (1): 5–12.

Greater Vancouver Transportation Authority. 2006. *Golden Ears Bridge Value for Money Report*. Vancouver: Greater Vancouver Transportation Authority.

Greenaway, John, Brian Salter, and Stella Hart. 2007. "How Policy Networks Can Damage Democratic Health: A Case Study in the Government of Governance." *Public Administration* 85 (3): 717–38.

Greenberg, Lee. 2011. "Siemens Wants in on Light Rail Project; Firm Pushes Ontario on Content Rules." *The Ottawa Citizen*, 6 July, A1.

Gregg, Judd. 2015. "GOP, Get Real on Health Care." *The Boston Globe*, 8 December, A11.

Greve, Carsten and Graeme Hodge. 2010. "Public-Private Partnerships and Public Governance Challenges." In *The New Public Governance? Emerging Perspectives on the Theory and Practice of Public Governance*, edited by Stephen P. Osborne, 149–62. London and New York: Routledge.

Greve, Henrich. R. 2011. "Fast and Expensive: The Diffusion of a Disappointing Innovation." *Strategic Management Journal* 32 (9): 949–68.

Griffith, Janice C. 1990. "Local Government Contracts: Escaping from the Governmental/Proprietary Maze." *Iowa Law Review* 75 (2): 277–380.

Grimsey, Darrin and Mervyn K. Lewis. 2004. *Public Private Partnerships: The Worldwide Revolution in Infrastructure Provision and Project Finance*. Cheltenham, UK; Northampton, MA: Edward Elgar Publishing.

– 2005. "Are Public Private Partnerships Value for Money? Evaluating Alternative Approaches and Comparing Academic and Practitioner Views." *Accounting Forum* 29 (4): 345–78.

Grossman, Peter Z. 2009. "U.S. Energy Policy and the Presumption of Market Failure." *Cato Journal* 29 (2): 295–317.

Hacker, Jacob S. 2004. "Privatizing Risk Without Privatizing the Welfare State: The Hidden Politics of Social Policy Retrenchment in the United States." *American Political Science Review* 98 (2): 243–60.

Hager, Mike 2011. "Canada Line Service Expanding." *The Vancouver Sun*, 8 August, A4.

Hakim, Simon, Paul Seidenstat, and Gary W. Bowman. 1996. "Review and Analysis of Privatization Efforts in Transportation." In *Privatizing Transportation Systems*, edited by Simon Hakim, Paul Seidenstat, and Gary W. Bowman, 3–24. Westport, CT: Praeger.

Halcrow Group Limited. 2003. "Richmond/Airport/Vancouver Rapid Transit Project Definition Phase." *Final Report on Ridership and Revenues*, January. London: Halcrow Group Limited.

Hall, Peter A. 1993. "Policy Paradigms, Social Learning, and the State: The Case of Economic Policymaking in Britain." *Comparative Politics* 25 (3): 275–96.

Hansen, Michael G. and Charles H. Levine. 1988. "The Centralization-Decentralization Tug-of-War in the New Executive Branch." In *Organizing Governance, Governing Organizations*, edited by Colin Campbell and B. Guy Peters, 255–82. Pittsburgh: University of Pittsburgh Press.

Haque, M. Shamsul. 2004. "Governance and Bureaucracy in Singapore: Contemporary Reforms and Implications." *International Political Science Review* 25 (2): 227–40.

Harcourt, Mike and Ken Cameron. 2007. *City Making in Paradise: Nine Decisions That Saved Vancouver*. Vancouver: Douglas and McIntyre Ltd.

Harding, Richard. 2001. "Private Prisons." *Crime and Justice* 28: 265–346.

Hart, Oliver. 2003. "Incomplete Contracts and Public Ownership: Remarks, and an Application to Public-Private Partnerships." *The Economic Journal* 113 (486): C69–76.

Hatzopoulou, M. and E.J. Miller 2007. "Institutional Integration for Sustainable Transportation Policy in Canada." *Transport Policy* 15 (3): 149–62.

Helderman, Jan-Kees, Frederik T. Schut, Tom E.D. van der Grinten, and Wynand P.M.M. van de Ven. 2005. "Market-Oriented Health Care Reforms and Policy Learning in the Netherlands." *Journal of Health Politics, Policy and Law* 30 (1–2): 189–209.

Hemerijck, Anton. 2013. *Changing Welfare States*. Oxford: Oxford University Press.

Hertting, Nils. 2007. "Mechanisms of Governance Network Formation – A Contextual Rational Choice Perspective." In *Theories of Democratic Network Governance*, edited by Eva Sørensen and Jacob Torfing, 43–60. Basingstoke, UK and New York: Palgrave Macmillan.

Hodge, Graeme. 2004. "The Risky Business of Public–Private Partnerships." *Australian Journal of Public Administration* 63 (4): 37–49.

Hodge, Graeme and Diana Bowman. 2004. "PPP Contractual Issues – Big Promises and Unfinished Business." In *Public-Private Partnerships: Policy and Experience*, edited by Abby Ghobadian, David Gallear, Nicholas O'Regan, and Howard Viney, 201–18. Basingstoke, UK and New York: Palgrave Macmillan.

Hollander, Robyn and Haig Patapan. 2007. "Pragmatic Federalism: Australian Federalism from Hawke to Howard." *Australian Journal of Public Administration* 66 (3): 280–97.

Horrigan, Darren. 1991. "Govt Airport Link 'A Flop.'" *Sydney Morning Herald*, 2 May, 4.

Hughes, Ted. 2003. *Richmond • Airport • Vancouver Rapid Transit Project (AVRTP) Report #1 of the Fairness Auditor*, 1 May.

Humpherson, Andrew. 1994. "Sydney Heliport Bill." *Full Day Hansard Transcript (Legislative Assembly)*, 3 March, Corrected Copy.

Humphries, David. 1998. "Carr Minister Set to Quit Over Travel Rorts Affair." *Sydney Morning Herald*, 30 April, 1.

Hutchens, Gareth and Lucy Macken. 2015. "Hockey Says More Homes Being Investigated." *Sydney Morning Herald*, 5 March, 2.

Hutton, Thomas A. 2012. "Multilevel Governance and Urban Development: A Vancouver Case Study." In *Sites of Governance: Multilevel Governance and Policy Making in Canada's Big Cities*, edited by Martin Horak and Robert Young, 263–98. Montreal and Kingston: McGill-Queen's University Press.

IBI Group. 2001. "Richmond-Airport-Vancouver Rapid Transit Project: Multiple Account Evaluation." *Final Report*, 16 April. Vancouver: IBI Group.

InTransit BC. 2006. "Detailed Design Consultation for Canada Line Stations." *Consultation Summary Report Prepared by National Public Relations on Behalf of InTransitBC*, November.

Ivens, Andy. 2011. "Susan Heyes Loses Court Award Battle." *The Vancouver Sun*, 21 October, A.21.

Jacobsen, Geesche. 2004. "So It's 2004: Take a Pill, Pay Your Way." *Sydney Morning Herald*, 1 January, 2.

Jenkins-Smith, Hank C. and Paul A. Sabatier. 1993. "The Dynamics of Policy-Oriented Learning." In *Policy Change and Learning: An Advocacy Coalition Approach*, edited by Paul A. Sabatier and Hank C. Jenkins-Smith, 41–56. Boulder, CO: Westview.

Jessop, Bob. 1998. "The Rise of Governance and the Risks of Failure: The Case of Economic Development." *International Social Science Journal* 50 (155): 29–45.

– 2000. "Governance Failure." In *The New Politics of British Local Governance*, edited by Gerry Stoker, 11–32. London and New York: Macmillan.

Johnston, Rita. 1990. "Estimates: Ministry of Transportation and Highways." *Official Report of Debates of the Legislative Assembly (Hansard)*, 17 July. Morning Sitting.

Jones, Joseph. 1984. *The Politics of Transport in Twentieth-Century France*. Montreal and Kingston: McGill-Queen's University Press.

Jones, Kathy. 2000. *Breakthrough: The Story of the Underground Rail Link to Sydney Airport*. Edgecliff, NSW: Focus Publishing.

Kazatchkine, Michel. 2014. "Russia's Ban on Methadone for Drug Users in Crimea Will Worsen the HIV/AIDS Epidemic and Risk Public Health." *British Medical Journal* 348: g3118.

Kerr, Donna H. 1976. "The Logic of 'Policy' and Successful Policies." *Policy Sciences* 7 (3): 351–63.

Kerr, Joseph and Nick O'Malley. 2003. "Costa Puts Up Cheaper Options for Train Link." *Sydney Morning Herald*, 4 June, 3.

Kiesel, Kristin, Jill J. McCluskey, and Sofia B. Villas-Boas. 2011. "Nutritional Labeling and Consumer Choices." *Annual Review of Resource Economics* 3 (1): 141–58.

Kinhill Engineers Pty Ltd. 1994. *New Southern Railway Environmental Impact Statement*. Sydney: State Rail Authority of New South Wales.

Kirk and Co. Consulting Ltd. 2003. *Consultation Summary Report: RAVp Community Consultation 2003*. Report for the Richmond Airport Vancouver Rapid Transit Project, 28 March.

Klijn, Erik-Hans and Joop F.M. Koppenjan. 2000. "Public Management and Policy Networks: Foundations of a Network Approach to Governance." *Public Management Review* 2 (2): 135–58.

Klijn, Erik-Hans and Geert R. Teisman. 2004. "Public-Private Partnership: The Right Form at the Wrong Moment? An Analysis of Institutional and Strategic Obstacles." In *Public-Private Partnerships: Policy and Experience*, edited by Abby Ghobadian, David Gallear, Nicholas

O'Regan, and Howard Viney, 147–61. Basingstoke, UK and New York: Palgrave Macmillan.

Knight, Elizabeth. 2000. "Private Face of Government." *Sydney Morning Herald*, 1 December, 23.

Knill, Christoph and Dirk Lehmkuhl. 2002. "Private Actors and the State: Internationalization and Changing Patterns of Governance." *Governance* 15 (1): 41–63.

Koppenjan, Joop F.M. 2007. "Consensus and Conflict in Policy Networks: Too Much or Too Little?" In *Theories of Democratic Network Governance*, edited by Eva Sørensen and Jacob Torfing, 133–52. Basingstoke, UK and New York: Palgrave Macmillan.

Koppenjan, Joop F.M. and Bert Enserink. 2009. "Public–Private Partnerships in Urban Infrastructures: Reconciling Private Sector Participation and Sustainability." *Public Administration Review* 69 (2): 284–96.

Koppenjan, Joop, Mirjam Kars, and Haiko van der Voort. 2009. "Vertical Politics in Horizontal Policy Networks: Framework Setting as Coupling Arrangement." *Policy Studies Journal* 37 (4): 769–92.

Krangle, Karenn. 2003. "Arbutus Fast-Bus Study Ordered by City Council." *The Vancouver Sun*, 14 March, B2.

Kushner, Joseph and David Siegel. 2003. "Effect of Municipal Amalgamations in Ontario on Political Representation and Accessibility." *Canadian Journal of Political Science* 36 (5): 1035–51.

Lahiri-Dutt, Kuntala. 2004. "'I Plan, You Participate': A Southern View of Community Participation in Urban Australia." *Community Development Journal* 39 (1): 13–27.

Langford, John. 1999. "Governance Challenges of Public-Private Partnerships." In *Collaborative Government: Is There a Canadian Way? New Directions Series Number 6*, edited by Susan Delacourt and Donald G. Lenihan, 105–11. Toronto: The Institute of Public Administration of Canada.

Langton, Brian. 1997. "Legislative Council – General Purpose Standing Committees, General Purpose Standing Committee No. 4, Monday 2 June 1997: Transport and Tourism." *Full Day Hansard Transcript (Legislative Council)*, 2 June, Corrected Copy.

Larriera, Alicia. 1991. "Second Harbour Tunnel On Govt Short List." *Sydney Morning Herald*, 29 April, 3.

Lee, Chung H. 1992. "The Government, Financial System, and Large Private Enterprises in the Economic Development of South Korea." *World Development* 20 (2): 187–97.

Lee, Jeff. 1988. "Ward System Referendum Defeated by Vancouver Voters." *The Vancouver Sun*, 21 November, A5.

– 2004. "Victoria Declares RAV Line Dead, Assails TransLink Board." *The Vancouver Sun*, 19 June, A1.

Lee, Jeff and Catherine Rolfsen. 2009. "Vancouver Begs for Olympic Loan; With Deadline Looming, Vancouver Needs to Borrow $458M to Finish Athletes' Village." *Edmonton Journal*, 13 January, A5.

Le Grand, Julian. 1987. "The Middle-Class Use of the British Social Services." In *Not Only the Poor: The Middle Classes and the Welfare State*, edited by Robert E. Goodin and Julian Le Grand, 91–107. London: Allen and Unwin.

– 1991. "The Theory of Government Failure." *British Journal of Political Science* 21 (4): 423–42.

Legrand, Timothy. 2012. "Overseas and Over Here: Policy Transfer and Evidence-Based Policy-Making." *Policy Studies* 33 (4): 329–48.

Levinson, David, Reinaldo C. Garcia, and Kathy Carlson. 2007. "A Framework for Assessing Public-Private Partnerships." In *Institutions and Sustainable Transport: Regulatory Reform in Advanced Economies*, edited by Piet Rietveld and Roger R. Stough, 285–304. Cheltenham, UK and Northampton, MA: Edward Elgar.

Levy, Sidney M. 2011. *Public-Private Partnerships: Case Studies on Infrastructure Development*. Reston, Virginia: American Society of Civil Engineers.

Lewis, Julie. 1990. "Airport-City Rail Link Plan." *Sydney Morning Herald*, 9 October, 9.

Lilley, Mick and Catherine de Giorgio. 2004. "Forum: Public-Private Partnerships: A Private-Sector Perspective." *Australian Accounting Review* 14 (2): 34–41.

Lingard, Bob. 2010. "Policy Borrowing, Policy Learning: Testing Times in Australian Schooling." *Critical Studies in Education* 51 (2): 129–47.

Lockwood, Steve. 2007. "Public and Private Roles in Transport Network Development." In *Institutions and Sustainable Transport: Regulatory Reform in Advanced Economies*, edited by Piet Rietveld and Roger R. Stough, 233–62. Cheltenham, UK; Northampton, MA: Edward Elgar Publishing.

Lodge, Martin. 2003. "Institutional Choice and Policy Transfer: Reforming British and German Railway Regulation." *Governance* 16 (2): 159–78.

Luba, Frank. 2005. "Money-Losing Millennium Line Falls Far Short of Targeted Ridership." *The Province*, 16 May, A4.

MacAvoy, Paul W., W.T. Stanbury, George Yarrow, and Richard J. Zeck-hauser. 2012. "Introduction." In *Privatization and State-Owned Enter-prises: Lessons from the United States, Great Britain and Canada*, edited by Paul W. MacAvoy, W.T. Stanbury, George Yarrow, and Richard J. Zeckhauser, 1–5. Boston: Kluwer Academic Publishers.

Marques, Rui Cunha and Sanford Berg. 2010. "Revisiting the Strengths and Limitations of Regulatory Contracts in Infrastructure Industries." *Journal of Infrastructure Systems* 16 (4): 334–42.

Marr, Garry. 2012. "Tougher Mortgage Rules Hit Their Mark; Real Estate Sector." *Financial Post*, 26 November, FP1.

Marsh, David and J.C. Sharman. 2009. "Policy Diffusion and Policy Transfer." *Policy Studies* 30 (3): 269–88.

Mayeda, Andrew. 2010. "Competition Push Behind Teleco Decision, Clement Says." *National Post*, 4 January, A6.

Mayntz, Renate. 1993. "Governing Failures and the Problem of Govern-ability: Some Comments on a Theoretical Paradigm." In *Modern Gov-ernance: New Government-Society Interactions*, edited by Jan Kooiman, 9–20. Newbury Park, CA, London, and New Delhi: Sage.

McClymont, Kate. 2007. "Council to Pay $2.9m for Canned Contract." *Sydney Morning Herald*, 29 March, 5.

McConnell, Allan. 2010. *Understanding Policy Success: Rethinking Public Policy*. Basingstoke, UK: Palgrave Macmillan.

McHardie, Daniel. 2011. "Highway Transforms into 'A Poisoned Chal-ice." *Canadian Broadcasting Corporation* 11 October. http://www.cbc.ca /news/canada/new-brunswick/highway-transforms-into-a-poisoned-chalice-1.1041422.

Meseguer, Covadonga. 2005. "Policy Learning, Policy Diffusion, and the Making of a New Order." *Annals of the American Academy of Political and Social Science* 598 (1): 67–82.

Mévellec, Anne. 2009. "Working the Political Field in Stormy Weather: A Mayor's Role in the Quebec Municipal Mergers." *Canadian Journal of Political Science* 42 (3): 773–92.

Migdal, Joel S. 1988. *Strong Societies and Weak States: State-Society Rela-tions and State Capabilities in the Third World*. Princeton, NJ: Princeton University Press.

Milmo, Dan. 2009. "Collapse of Tube Contractor Metronet Could Cost Taxpayer £410m." *The Guardian*, 5 June. http://www.theguardian.com /business/2009/jun/05/metronet-london-underground-ppp.

Mitchell, Andrew D. and David M. Studdert. 2012. "Plain Packaging of

Tobacco Products in Australia: A Novel Regulation Faces Legal Challenge." *Journal of the American Medical Association* 307 (3): 261–2.

Moavenzadeh, F. and M.J. Markow. 2007. *Moving Millions: Transport Strategies for Sustainable Development in Megacities*. Dordrecht, Netherlands: Springer.

Mols, Frank. 2010. "Harnessing Market Competition in PPP Procurement: The Importance of Periodically Taking a Strategic View." *Australian Journal of Public Administration* 69 (2): 229–44.

Moore, Matthew. 1990. "Airport Rail Link Go-Ahead; The Go-Ahead For Runway Three." *Sydney Morning Herald*, 20 September, 4.

Moore, Matthew and Bernard Lagan. 1989. "Arriving Next on Platform 1: Clean, Efficient Trains." *Sydney Morning Herald*, 2 May, 1.

Morris, Linda. 1994a. "Airport Rail Link Doubt After Subsidy Refused." *Sydney Morning Herald*, 27 July, 4.

– 1994b. "Professor Calls Airport Rail Link a 'Bad Deal." *Sydney Morning Herald*, 19 September, 9.

– 1995a. "Langton Removes State Rail Chief." *Sydney Morning Herald*, 28 April, 3.

– 1995b. "Airport's Rail Link Bill May Be $716m." *Sydney Morning Herald*, 13 October, 5.

– 1996a. "Rail Link Costs Taxpayers Extra $27m." *Sydney Morning Herald*, 17 May, 7.

– 1996b. "Restructure of State Rail Grinds to Halt." *Sydney Morning Herald*, 22 June, 17.

– 1997. "Senior Men Axed in Rail Shake-up." *Sydney Morning Herald*, 16 May, 3.

– 2002. "A Capital Idea." *Sydney Morning Herald*, 6 July, 33.

Mossberger, Karen and Harold Wolman. 2003. "Policy Transfer as a Form of Prospective Policy Evaluation: Challenges and Recommendations." *Public Administration Review* 63 (4): 428–40.

Mustafa, Amira. 1999. "Public-Private Partnership: An Alternative Institutional Model for Implementing the Private Finance Initiative in the Provision of Transport Infrastructure." *Journal of Project Finance* 5 (1): 56–71.

Mylvaganam, Chandran and Sandford Borins. 2004. *"If you build it ...": Business, Government, and Ontario's Electronic Toll Highway*. Toronto: Centre for Public Management, University of Toronto.

Nafziger, James A.R. and Angela M. Wanak. 2009. "United Parcel Service, Inc., V. Government Of Canada: An Example of a Trend in the

Arbitration of NAFTA-Related Investment Disputes." *Willamette Journal of International Law and Dispute Resolution* 17 (1): 49–79.

New South Wales. 1993. *Integrated Transport Strategy for Greater Sydney: A First Release for Public Discussion, October*. Sydney, NSW: City Planning Department.

– 1994. *New Southern Railway: Urban Planning Strategy for the New Southern Railway*. Sydney: New South Wales Government Department of Planning.

– 2014. *Removing or Reducing Station Access Fees at Sydney Airport: Report of the General Purpose Standing Committee No. 3*. Sydney: New South Wales Parliament.

Newman, Joshua. 2014. "Measuring Policy Success: Case Studies from Canada and Australia." *Australian Journal of Public Administration* 73 (2): 192–205.

Newman, Joshua and Malcolm G. Bird. 2017. "British Columbia's Fast Ferries and Sydney's Airport Link: Partisan Barriers to Learning from Policy Failure." *Policy and Politics* 45 (1): 71–85.

Newman, Joshua and Brian W. Head. 2015. "Categories of Failure in Climate Change Mitigation Policy in Australia." *Public Policy and Administration* 30 (3–4): 342–58.

Ng, A. and Martin Loosemore. 2007. "Risk Allocation in the Private Provision of Public Infrastructure." *International Journal of Project Management* 25 (1): 66–76.

Nisar, Tahir. M. 2007. "Value for Money Drivers in Public Private Partnership Schemes." *International Journal of Public Sector Management* 20 (2): 147–56.

Nixon, Sherrill. 2006. "A Few More Board the Airport Train." *Sydney Morning Herald*, 16 March, 3.

Oakley, Deirdre. 2006. "The American Welfare State Decoded: Uncovering the Neglected History of Public-Private Partnerships." *City and Community* 5 (3): 243–67.

Ohemeng, Frank K. and John K. Grant. 2008. "When Markets Fail to Deliver: An Examination of the Privatization and De-Privatization of Water and Wastewater Services Delivery in Hamilton, Canada." *Canadian Public Administration* 51 (3): 475–99.

O'Neill, Peter. 2004. "Ottawa Will Add $150 million to RAV Project." *The Vancouver Sun*, 16 April, A1.

Oppen, Maria, Detlef Sack, and Alexander Wegener. 2005. "German Public-Private Partnerships in Personal Social Services: New Directions in a Corporatist Environment." In *The Challenge of Public-Private Partnerships*, edited by Graeme Hodge and Carsten Greve, 269–89. Cheltenham, UK and Northampton, MA: Edward Elgar.

Oum, Tae H., Nicole Adler, and Chunyan Yu. 2006. "Privatization, Corporatization, Ownership Forms and Their Effects on the Performance of the World's Major Airports." *Journal of Air Transport Management* 12 (3): 109–21.

Padova, Allison. 2007. *Airport Governance Reform in Canada and Abroad*. Parliamentary Information and Research Service, Economics Division, 5 September. Ottawa: Library of Parliament.

Painter, Martin. 2001. "Multi-Level Governance and the Emergence of Collaborative Federal Institutions in Australia." *Policy and Politics* 29 (2): 137–50.

Papajohn, Dean, Qingbin Cui, and Mehmet Emre Bayraktar. 2011. "Public-Private Partnerships in U.S. Transportation: Research Overview and a Path Forward." *Journal of Management in Engineering* 27 (3): 126–35.

Patashnik, Eric. 2003. "After the Public Interest Prevails: The Political Sustainability of Policy Reform." *Governance* 16 (2): 203–34.

Perl, Anthony. 1994. "Public Enterprise as an Expression of Sovereignty: Reconsidering the Origin of Canadian National Railways." *Canadian Journal of Political Science* 27 (1): 23–52.

Perl, Anthony and James Dunn Jr. 2007. "Reframing Automobile Fuel Economy Policy in North America: The Politics of Punctuating a Policy Equilibrium." *Transport Reviews* 27 (1): 1–35.

Perl, Anthony and Joshua Newman. 2012. "Institutionalized Inhibition: Examining Constraints on Climate Change Policy Capacity in the Transport Departments of Ontario and British Columbia, Canada." *Canadian Political Science Review* 6 (1): 87–99.

Pierre, Jon and B. Guy Peters. 2000. *Governance, Politics and the State*. New York: St. Martin's Press.

Plamondon, Aaron. 2010. *The Politics of Procurement: Military Acquisition in Canada and the Sea King Helicopter*. Vancouver: UBC Press.

Pongsiri, Nutavoot. 2002. "Regulation and Public-Private Partnerships." *International Journal of Public Sector Management* 16 (6): 487–95.

Poschmann, Finn. 2003. *Private Means to Public Ends: The Future of Public-Private Partnerships*. Toronto: C.D. Howe Institute.

PricewaterhouseCoopers. 2003. "RAVP Project Definition: Report on Financial Feasibility." Executive Summary, February.

Quaglia, Lucia. 2012. "The 'Old' and 'New' Politics of Financial Services Regulation in the European Union." *New Political Economy* 17 (4): 515–35.

Quiggin, John. 2004. "Risk, PPPs and the Public Sector Comparator." *Australian Accounting Review* 14 (33): 51–61.

– 2005. "Public–Private Partnerships: Options for Improved Risk Allocation." *The Australian Economic Review* 38 (4): 445–50.

RailCorp. 2005. *Restated Stations Agreement (2005) New Southern Railway / New Southern Railway Settlement Deed / Global Amending Deed / Deed Of Release: Contracts Summary, November.* Sydney: Railcorp.

RAV Project Management Ltd. 2003. "Project Definition Report." Richmond/Airport/Vancouver Rapid Transit Project Draft Report for Public Consultation, 27 February.

– 2004a. *Request for Proposals for the Richmond • Airport • Vancouver Rapid Transit Project.* Conformed Request for Proposals, 23 January.

– 2004b. *Request for Proposals for the Richmond • Airport • Vancouver Rapid Transit Project: Report of the Evaluation Committee.* Executive Summary, 13 April.

– 2004c. "Ravco Selects Two Proponents From Three." *Richmond Airport Vancouver Rapid Transit Project News Release,* 31 March.

– 2005a. *Amended and Restated RAV Concession Agreement for the Richmond•Airport•Vancouver Rapid Transit Project.* Execution Copy: 29 July.

– 2005b. *Environmental Assessment Certificate T05-01: Design and Construction Method Changes to the Cambie Portion of the Vancouver Segment.* Report prepared for the BC Environmental Assessment Office, 13 September.

– 2005c. *RavP Preliminary Design Consultation.* Vancouver: RAV Project Office.

– 2005d. *Responses to Environmental Assessment Certificate Application and Application Supplement: Agency Comments.* Report prepared for the BC Environmental Assessment Office, 23 March.

– 2005e. "RAV Line Construction Phase Starts RAVCO and InTransitBC Reach Final Agreement." *Information Bulletin: Bulletin No. 9,* 2 August.

Read, Nicholas, Ayesha Bhatty, and Jim Beatty. 2004. "RAV Line Resurrected as B.C. Offers to Cover Overruns." *The Vancouver Sun,* 11 June, A1.

Regeczi, David. 2008. *Private Equity; Public Principle: Evaluating the Legitimacy and Sustainability of Public-Private Partnerships.* Enschede, Netherlands: University of Twente Press.

Rephann, Terance. J. 1993. "Highway Investment and Regional Econom-
    ic Development: Decision Methods and Empirical Foundations."
    Urban Studies 30 (2): 437–50.
Rhodes, R.A.W. 2006. "Policy Network Analysis." In *The Oxford Handbook
    of Public Policy*, edited by Michael Moran, Martin Rein, and Robert E.
    Goodin, 425–47. New York: Oxford University Press.
Rietveld, Piet and Roger R. Stough. 2007. "Institutions and Regulatory
    Reform in Transport: An Introduction." In *Institutions and Sustainable
    Transport: Regulatory Reform in Advanced Economies*, edited by Piet
    Rietveld and Roger R. Stough, 1–14. Cheltenham, UK; Northampton,
    MA: Edward Elgar Publishing.
Rose, Richard. 1991. "What Is Lesson-Drawing?" *Journal of Public Policy* 2
    (1): 3–30.
– 1993. *Lesson-Drawing in Public Policy: A Guide to Learning Across Time
    and Space*. Chatham, NJ: Chatham House.
– 2004. *Learning from Comparative Public Policy: A Practical Guide*. Lon-
    don & New York: Routledge.
Rosenau, Pauline Vaillancourt. 2000. "The Strengths and Weaknesses of
    Public-Private Partnerships." In *Public-Private Policy Partnerships*, edited
    by Pauline Vaillancourt Rosenau, 217–41. Cambridge, MA: MIT Press.
Ruffilli, Dean C. 2010. "Federal Support for Bus Rapid Transit and Light
    Rail Transit Systems in Canada." *Parliamentary Information and
    Research Service, Industry, Infrastructure and Resources Division. Publica-
    tion No. 2010-64-E, 16 September 2010*. Ottawa: Library of Parliament.
Rufín, Carlos and Miguel Rivera-Santos. 2012. "Between Commonweal
    and Competition: Understanding the Governance of Public–Private
    Partnerships." *Journal of Management* 38 (5): 1634–54.
Sanatani, Suromitra. 2007. *Review of Canada Line Business Support Pro-
    grams*. Report to Canada Line Rapid Transit Inc., 20 September.
Sancton, Andrew 2012. "The Urban Agenda." In *Canadian Federalism:
    Performance, Effectiveness and Legitimacy, Third Edition*, edited by Her-
    man Bakvis and Grace Skogstad, 302–19. Don Mills, ON: Oxford Uni-
    versity Press.
Saulwick, Jacob. 2011a. "Some Commuters Get Cheaper Travel But Oth-
    ers Miss Out." *Sydney Morning Herald*, 3 March, 6.
– 2011b. "Ticket Price Drop Leads to Huge Jump in Rail Travel." *Sydney
    Morning Herald*, 9 June, 3.
– 2011c. "Airport Link Contract Keeps Buses Out of Service." *Sydney
    Morning Herald*, 23 August, 3.

Savas, E.S. 2000. *Privatization and Public-Private Partnerships*. New York: Chatham House.

Sawyer, Malcolm. 2009. "Private Finance Initiative and Public Private Partnerships: The Key Issues." In *Critical Essays on the Privatization Experience*, edited by Philip Arestis and Malcolm Sawyer, 39–74. Basingstoke (England); New York: Palgrave Macmillan.

Scardilli, Adrian. 2000. "Casual Remark Started Rail Deal." *The Sun Herald*, 21 May, 7.

Schlosser, Eric. 1998. "The Prison-Industrial Complex." *The Atlantic Monthly* 282 (6): December, 51–77.

Searle, Glen. 1999. "New Roads, New Rail Lines, New Profits: Privatisation and Sydney's Recent Transport Development." *Urban Policy and Research* 17 (2): 111–21.

Self, Peter. 1977. *Administrative Theories and Politics 2nd Edition*. London: George Allen and Unwin.

Shantz, Jeffrey. 2011. "Discrimination Against Latin American Workers During Pre-Olympic Games Construction in Vancouver." *Employee Responsibilities and Rights Journal* 23 (1): 75–80.

Shaoul, Jean. 2009. "The Political Economy of the Private Finance Initiative." In *Critical Essays on the Privatization Experience*, edited by Philip Arestis and Malcolm Sawyer, 1–38. Basingstoke, UK and New York: Palgrave Macmillan.

Shaoul, Jean, Anne Stafford, and Pamela Stapleton. 2012. "Accountability and Corporate Governance of Public Private Partnerships." *Critical Perspectives on Accounting* 23 (3): 213–29.

Siemiatycki, Matti. 2006. "Implications of Private-Public Partnerships on the Development of Urban Public Transit Infrastructure: The Case of Vancouver, Canada." *Journal of Planning Education and Research* 26 (2): 137–51.

– 2007. "What's the Secret? Confidentiality in Planning Infrastructure Using Public/Private Partnerships." *Journal of the American Planning Association* 73 (4): 388–403.

– 2010. "Delivering Transportation Infrastructure Through Public-Private Partnerships." *Journal of the American Planning Association* 76 (1): 43–58.

Siemiatycki, Matti and Naeem Farooqi. 2012. "Value for Money and Risk in Public–Private Partnerships." *Journal of the American Planning Association* 78 (3): 286–99.

Simmons, Beth A. and Zachary Elkins. 2004. "The Globalization of Liberalization: Policy Diffusion in the International Political Economy." *American Political Science Review* 98 (1): 171–89.

Simon, Herbert. 1972. "Theories of Bounded Rationality." In *Decision and Organization: A Volume in Honor of Jacob Marschak*, edited by C.B. McGuire and Roy Radner, 161–76. New York: North Holland Publishing.

Sinoski, Kelly. 2010. "Canada Line Ridership Picks Up Speed; Rapid Transit Route Reaches 100,000 Passengers a Day Three Years Earlier than Expected." *The Vancouver Sun*, 14 August, A12.

Skelton, Chad. 2004. "B.C. Enables Fight Bylaw: Vancouver Charter to be Amended." *The Vancouver Sun*, 14 May, B6.

Sørensen Eva and Jacob Torfing. 2005. "Network Governance and Post-Liberal Democracy." *Administrative Theory and Praxis* 27 (2): 197–237.

– 2007a. "Introduction: Governance Network Research: Towards a Second Generation." In *Theories of Democratic Network Governance*, edited by Eva Sørensen and Jacob Torfing, 1–21. Basingstoke, UK and New York: Palgrave Macmillan.

– 2007b. "Theoretical Approaches to Governance Network Failure." In *Theories of Democratic Network Governance*, edited by Eva Sørensen and Jacob Torfing, 95–110. Basingstoke, UK and New York: Palgrave Macmillan.

Spaxman Consulting Group. 2003. *Richmond – Airport – Vancouver Rapid Transit Project: Station Location Review, June 2003*. Vancouver: Spaxman Consulting Group.

Sperling, Daniel. 2001. "Public-Private Technology R&D Partnerships: Lessons from US Partnership for a New Generation of Vehicles." *Transport Policy* 8 (4): 247–56.

Steffenhagen, Janet. 2004. "RAV Foes Promote Light Rail Line." *The Vancouver Sun*, 21 June, B1.

Stoker, Gerry. 1998. "Governance as Theory: Five Propositions." *International Social Science Journal* 50 (155): 17–28.

Stone, Diane. 1999. "Learning Lessons and Transferring Policy Across Time, Space and Disciplines." *Politics* 19 (1): 51–9.

– 2004. "Transfer Agents and Global Networks in the 'Transnationalization' of Policy." *Journal of European Public Policy* 11 (3): 545–66.

Strelioff, Wayne. 2004. "Auditor General Financial Statement Audit Coverage Plan." *2004 Legislative Session, 5th Session, 37th Parliament. Select Standing Committee On Public Accounts, Monday, 22 November*.

Studlar, Donley T. 2006. "Tobacco Control Policy Instruments in a Shrinking World: How Much Policy Learning?" *International Journal of Public Administration* 29 (4–6): 367–96.

Synovate. 2003. *RAV Rapid Transit Study*. Report prepared for Richmond Airport Vancouver Rapid Transit, 20 March.

– 2004. *Survey Results On Public-Sector Involvement and RAV Design Topic Objectives*. Report prepared for Richmond Airport Vancouver Rapid Transit, 3 May.

TD Bank Financial Group. 2006. "Creating the Winning Conditions for Public-Private Partnerships (P3s) in Canada." *TD Economics Special Report*, 22 June 2006. Toronto: TD Bank Financial Group.

Teisman, Geert R. and Erik-Hans Klijn. 2002. "Partnership Arrangements: Governmental Rhetoric or Governance Scheme?" *Public Administration Review* 62 (2): 197–205.

Telliford, George T. 2009. *Public-Private Transportation Partnerships Around the World*. New York: Nova Science Publishers, Inc.

Thatcher, Mark. 1998. "The Development of Policy Network Analyses: From Modest Origins to Overarching Frameworks." *Journal of Theoretical Politics* 10 (4): 389–416.

Thériault, Luc. 2006. "The National Post and the Nanny State: Framing the Child Care Debate in Canada." *Canadian Review of Social Policy* 56: 140–48.

Tiernan, Anne. 2008. "The Council for the Australian Federation: A New Structure of Australian Federalism." *Australian Journal of Public Administration* 67 (2): 122–34.

Toulin, Alan. 1999. "Canada Post, Purolator Too Cosy, Rivals Charge 'A Virtual Subsidiary'; Association Wants Competition Bureau to Investigate." *National Post*, 23 April, C06.

Trampusch, Christine and André Mach. 2011. "The Swiss Political Economy in Comparative Perspective." In *Switzerland in Europe: Continuity and Change in the Swiss Political Economy*, edited by Christine Trampusch and André Mach, 11–25. Abingdon, UK: Routledge.

TransLink Commission. 2009. *Order Number, 09-02: Reasons for Decision on TransLink's Application of October 29 2009 For a Canada Line YVR Add Fare*. Comox, BC: South Coast British Columbia Regional Transportation Commission.

United Nations Economic Commission for Europe. 2008. *Guidebook on*

Promoting Good Governance in Public-Private Partnerships. New York and Geneva: United Nations.

Van Waarden, Frans. 1992. "Dimensions and Types of Policy Networks." *European Journal of Political Research* 21 (1–2): 29–52.

Van Zwanenberg, Patrick and Erik Millstone. 2003. "BSE: A Paradigm of Policy Failure." *The Political Quarterly* 74 (1): 27–37.

Vining, Aidan R. and Anthony E. Boardman. 2008. "Public-Private Partnerships in Canada: Theory and Evidence." *Canadian Public Administration* 51 (1): 9–44.

Vining, Aidan R. and David L. Weimer. 1990. "Government Supply and Government Production Failure: A Framework Based on Contestability." *Journal of Public Policy* 10 (1): 1–22.

Wainwright, Robert. 2000a. "Safety in Numbers as Struggling Airport Rail Line Cuts Fares for Group Travellers." *Sydney Morning Herald*, 16 August, 3.

– 2000b. "Chief's Sacking Signals Start of Rail Reform." *Sydney Morning Herald*, 31 October, 3.

– 2000c. "Taxpayers Billed $15m for Struggling Rail Link." *Sydney Morning Herald*, 17 November, 3.

– 2000d. "Taxpayers Face Bill After Airport Link Fails on Loan." *Sydney Morning Herald*, 22 November, 1.

– 2000e. "Taxpayer Became a Passenger as Debt-Laden Ghost Train Ran off the Rails." *Sydney Morning Herald*, 22 November, 10.

Wainwright, Robert and Ellen Connolly. 2000. "Rail Purge: Another Supremo's Head to Roll." *Sydney Morning Herald*, 2 November, 7.

Wallis, Joe and Brian Dollery. 2002. "Wolf's Model: Government Failure and Public Sector Reform in Advanced Industrial Democracies." *Review of Policy Research* 19 (1): 177–203.

Walker, R.G. 1994. *Sydney's Airport Link: Anatomy of a Deal*. Sydney: Public Sector Research Centre.

Walsh, James I. 2006. "Policy Failure and Policy Change: British Security Policy After the Cold War." *Comparative Political Studies* 39 (4): 490–518.

Watkins, John. 2005. "Airport Rail Link." *Legislative Assembly, Thursday 13 October 2005*.

Watson, David. 2003. "The Rise and Rise of Public Private Partnerships: Challenges for Public Accountability." *Australian Accounting Review* 13 (3): 2–14.

Webb, Kernaghan. 2005. "Sustainable Governance in the Twenty-First Century: Moving Beyond Instrument Choice." In *Designing Government: From Instruments to Governance*, edited by Pearl Eliadis, Margaret M. Hill, and Michael Howlett, 242–80. Montreal and Kingston: McGill-Queen's University Press.

Weber, Max. (1921) 1948. "Politics as a Vocation." In *From Max Weber: Essays in Sociology*, edited by Hans Gerth and C. Wright Mills, 77–128. New York: Oxford University Press.

Weimer, David and Aidan R. Vining. 2011. *Policy Analysis: Concepts and Practice, 5th edition*. Upper Saddle River, NJ: Pearson Prentice Hall.

Western Transportation Ministers Council. 2005. *Western Canada Transportation Infrastructure Strategy for an Economic Network: A Time for Vision and Leadership*. March.

Williams, Robert, David Greig, and Ian Wallis. 2005. *Results of Railway Privatization in Australia and New Zealand*. Washington, DC: World Bank.

Winston, Clifford. 2000. "Government Failure in Urban Transportation." *Fiscal Studies* 20 (4): 403–25.

Wolf, Charles Jr. 1987. "Market and Non-Market Failures: Comparison and Assessment." *Journal of Public Policy* 7 (1): 43–70.

– 1988: *Markets or Governments: Choosing Between Imperfect Alternatives*. Cambridge, MA and London: MIT Press.

Yaffe, Barbara. 2010. "Prime Minister Hopes Olympic Glow Reflects on Tories." *The Vancouver Sun*, 2 March, A5.

Yescombe, E.R. 2007. *Public-Private Partnerships: Principles of Policy and Finance*. Burlington, MA: Elsevier.

Yuan, Jingfeng, Alex Yajun Zeng, Miroslaw J. Skibniewski, and Qiming Li. 2009. "Selection of Performance Objectives and Key Performance Indicators in Public–Private Partnership Projects to Achieve Value for Money." *Construction Management and Economics* 27 (3): 253–70.

YVR. 2005. "YVR Funding Agreement (Restated) among Greater Vancouver Transportation Authority and Vancouver International Airport Authority and RAV Project Management Ltd. concerning the Richmond • Airport • Vancouver Rapid Transit Project." YVR Funding Agreement, 24 January.

Zhang, Xueqing. 2005. "Critical Success Factors for Public–Private Partnerships in Infrastructure Development." *Journal of Construction Engineering and Management* 131 (1): 3–14.

COURT DECISIONS

Heyes v. City of Vancouver 2009 BCSC 651
Susan Heyes Inc. (Hazel & Co.) v. South Coast BC Transportation Authority
2011 BCCA 77
Truth About Motorways v. Macquarie [2000] HCA 11

LEGISLATION

Greater Vancouver Transportation Authority Act 1998 (now titled South
Coast British Columbia Transportation Authority Act 1998)

Index